AF574183

## LETTER XXIII.

Palermo, June 30th.

THE account the people here give of the Sirocc, or South-eaſt wind, is truly aſtoniſhing; we were complaining to-day, at the viceroy's, of the violence of the heat, the thermometer being at 79.—They aſſured us, that if we ſtaid till the end of next month, we ſhould probably look on this as pleaſant cool weather; adding, that if we had once experienced the Sirocc, all other weather will appear temperate.—I aſked to what degree the thermometer commonly roſe during this wind; but found to my aſtoniſhment, that there was no ſuch inſtrument in uſe amongſt them: however, the violence of it, they aſſure us, is altogether incredible; and that thoſe who had remained many years in Spain and Malta, had never felt any heat in theſe countries to compare to it.—How it happens to be more violent in Palermo than any other part of Sicily, is a myſtery that ſtill remains to be unfolded. Several treatiſes have been writ

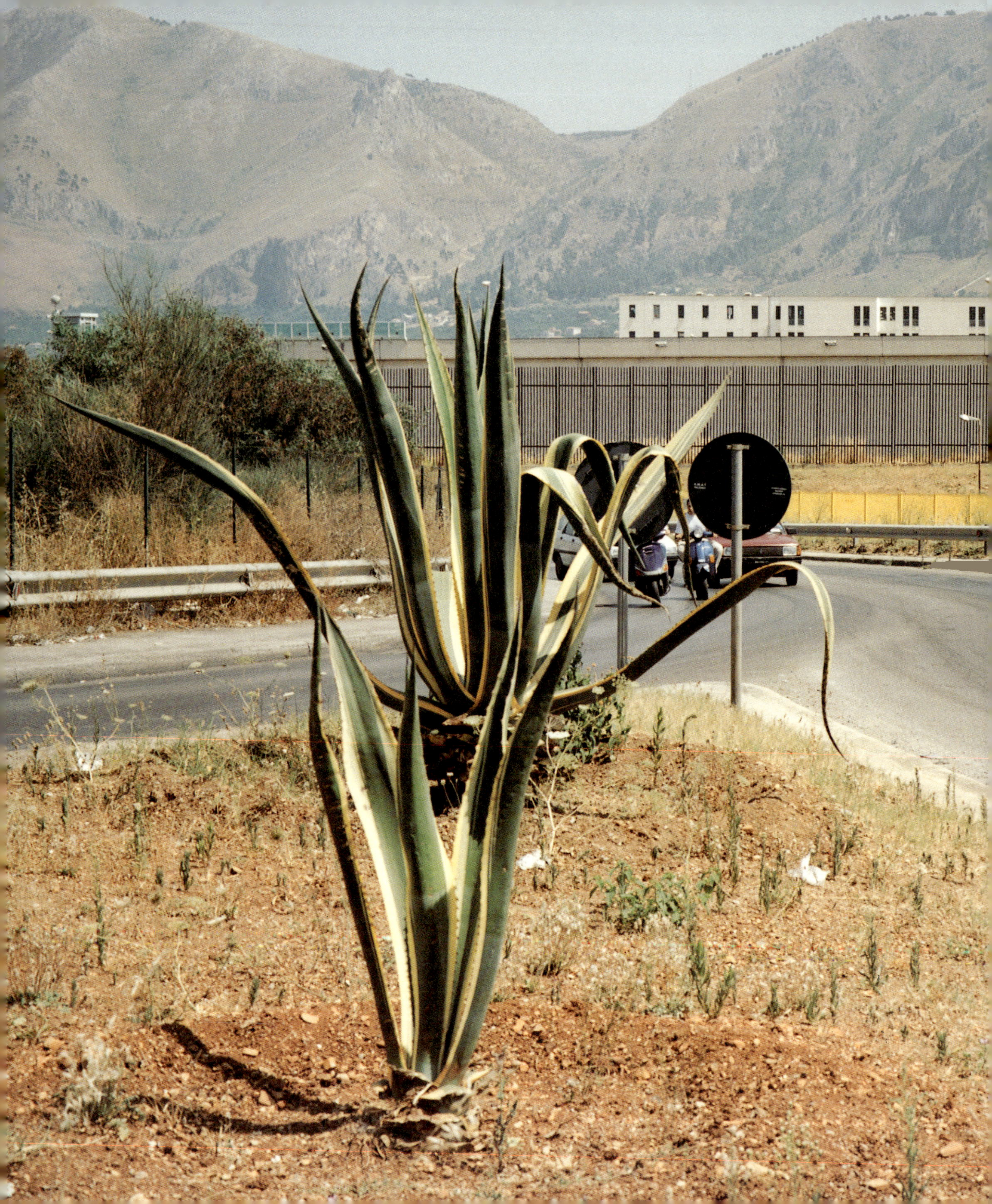

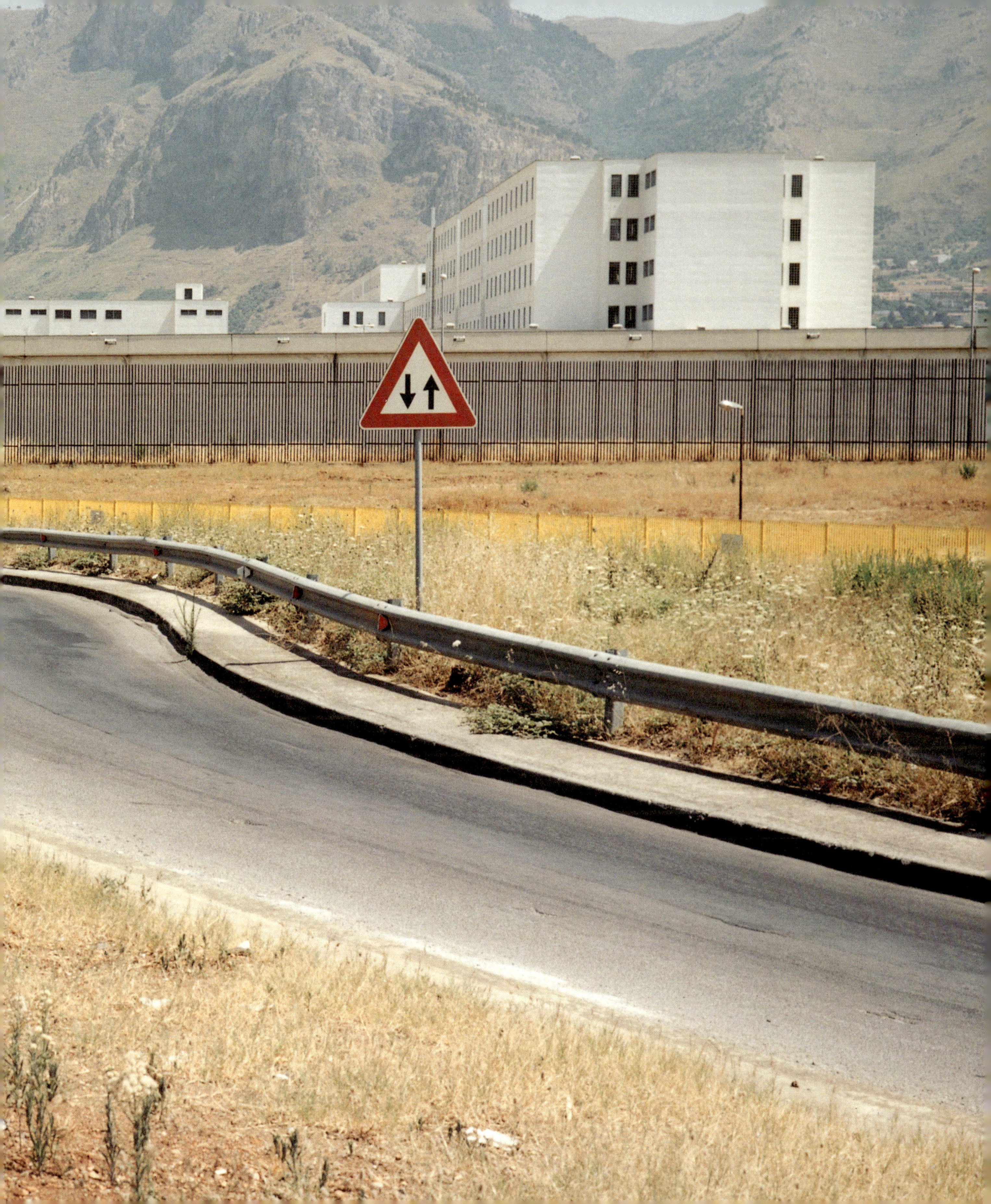

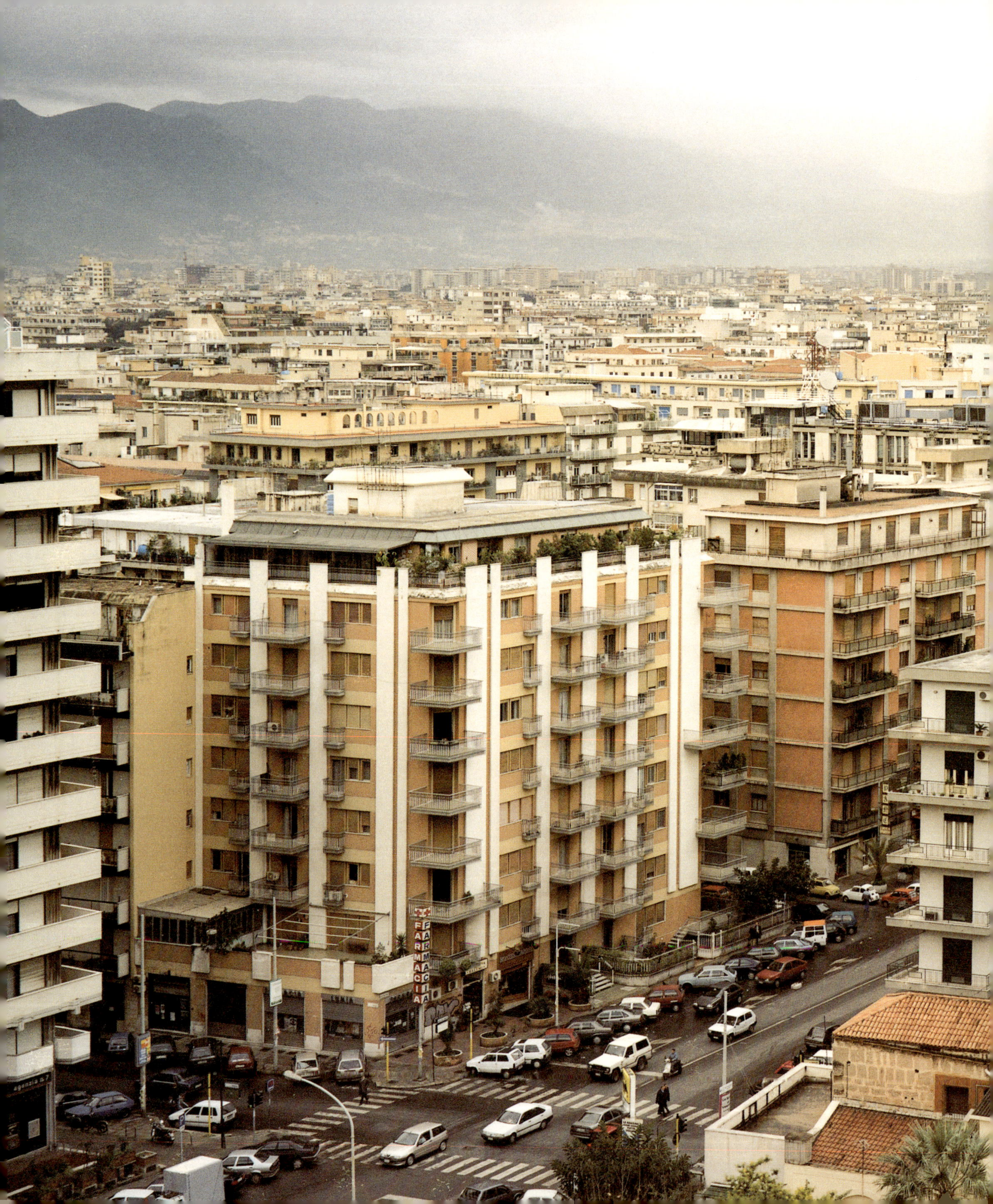
FARMACIA

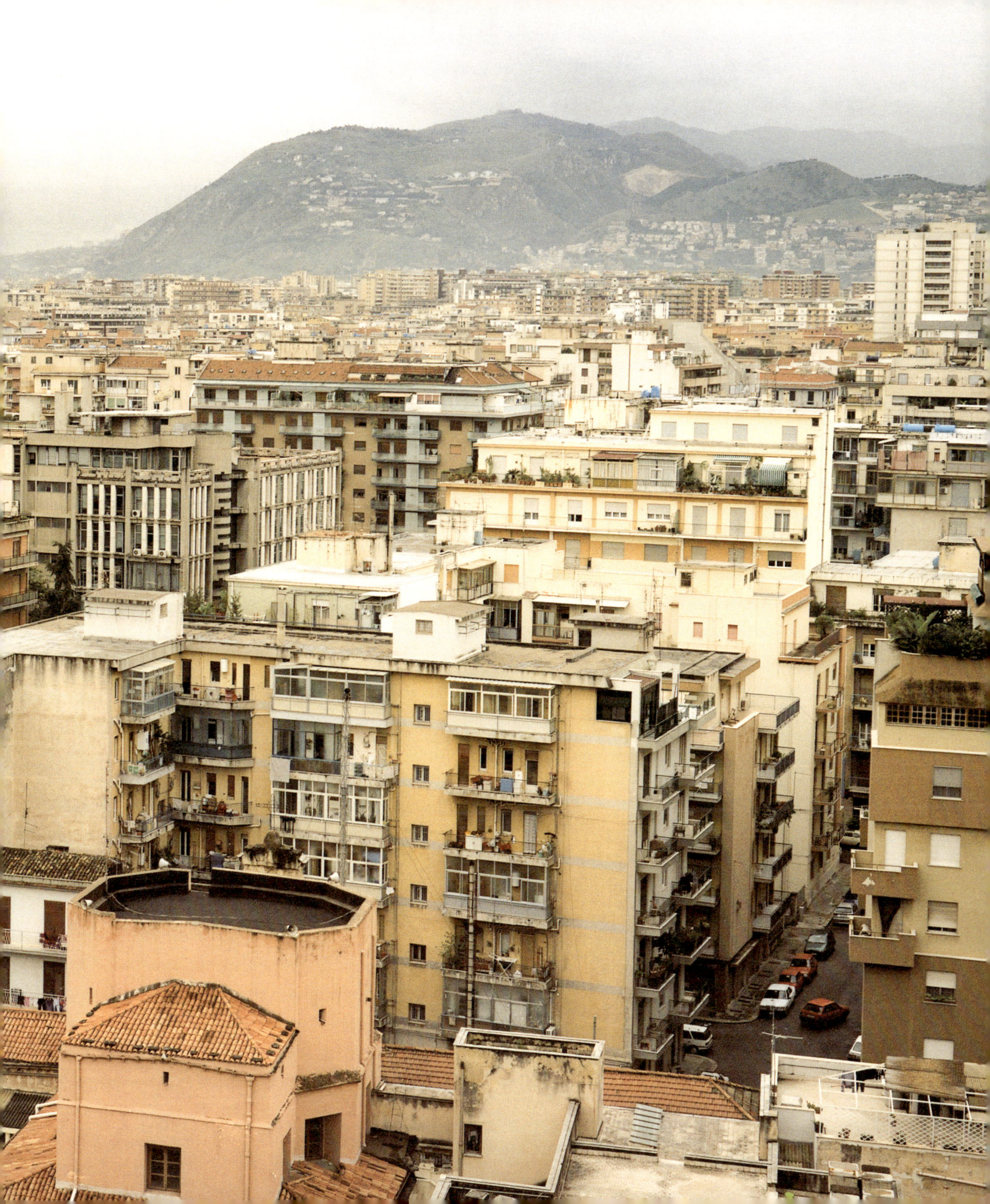

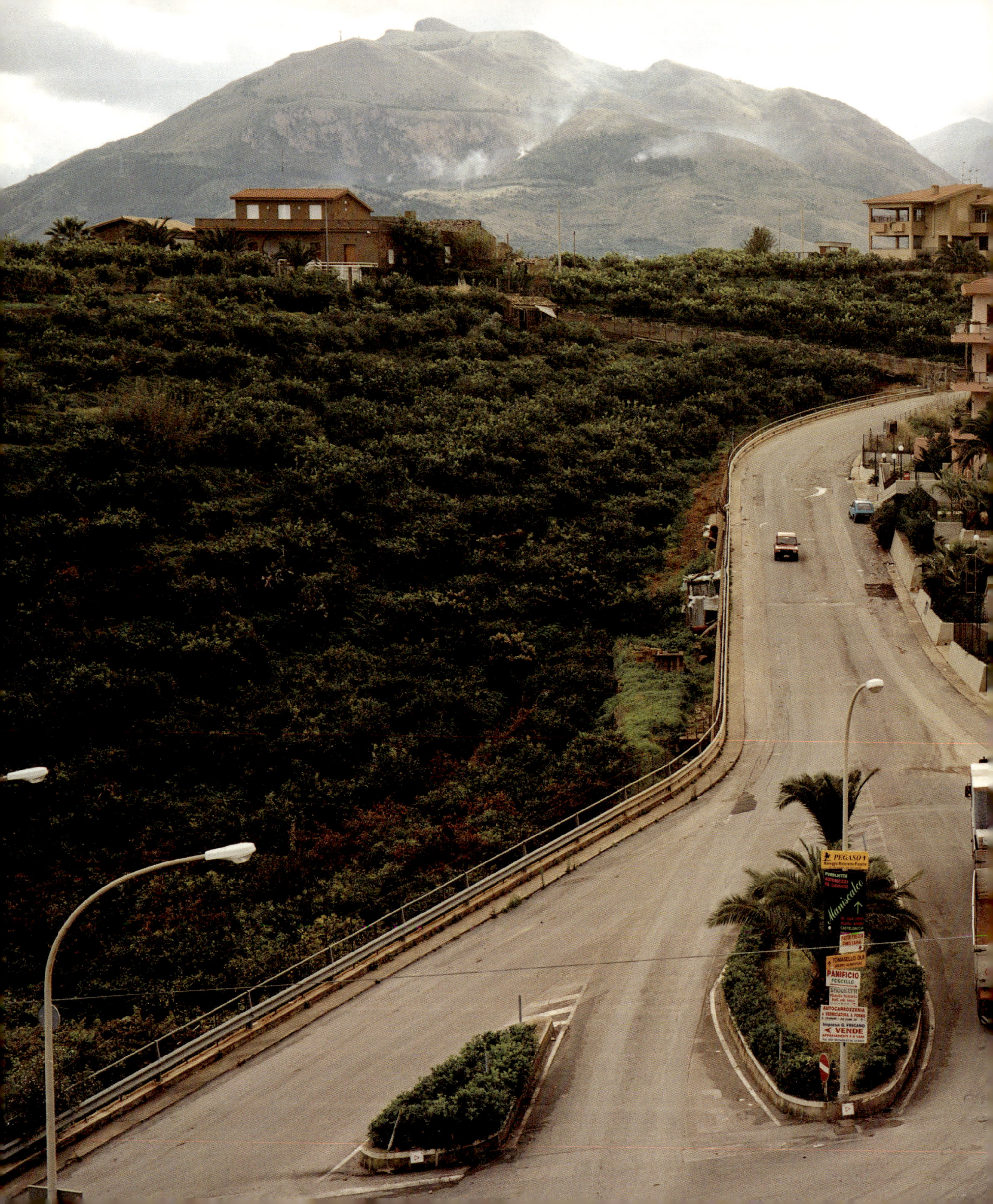
PEGASO
Maniscalco
CASTELDACCIA
TOMASELLO OLB
PANIFICIO
PORCELLO
AUTOCARROZZERIA
Impresa G. FRICANO
VENDE

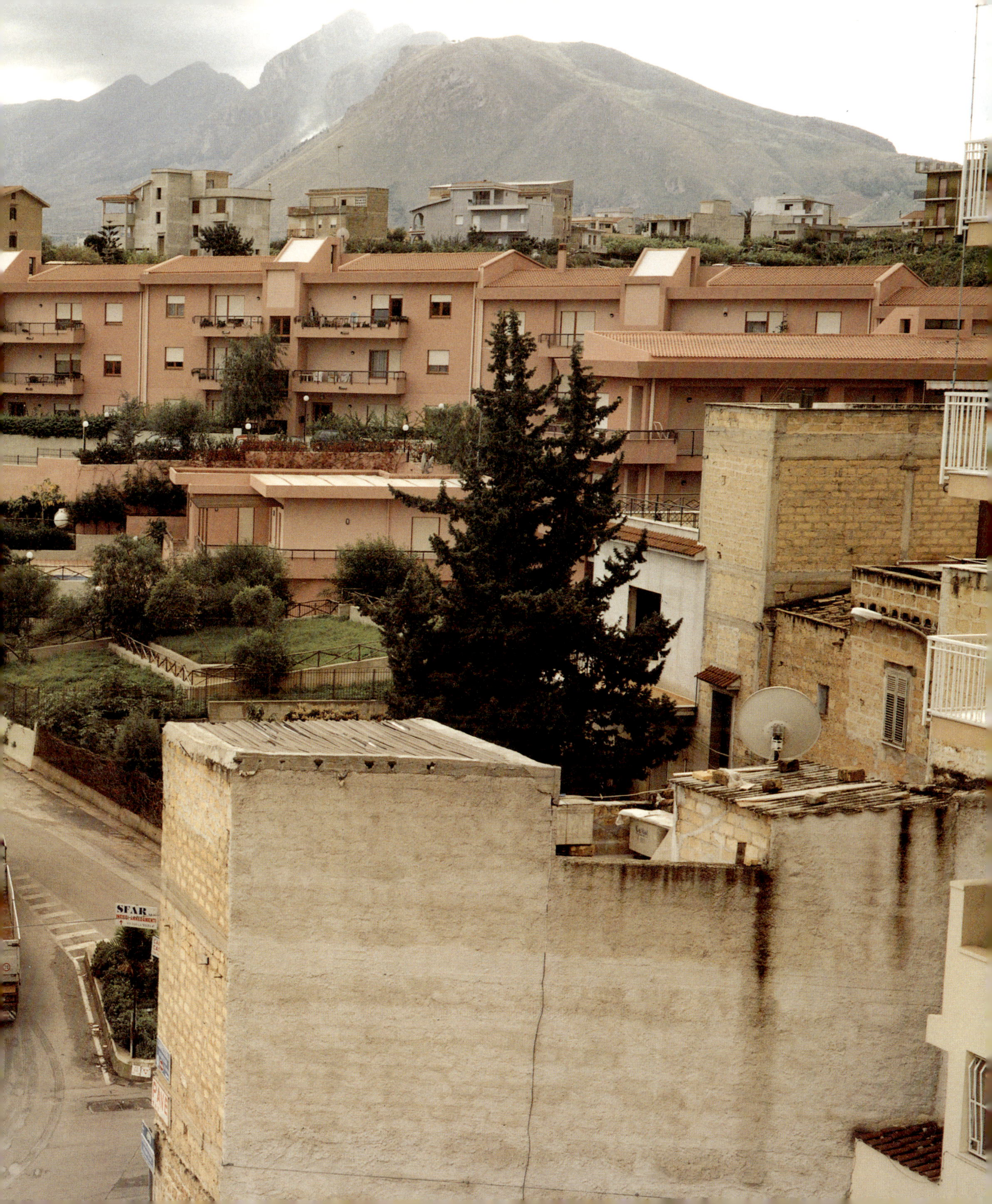
SFAR

Opening Page:
Letter from Patrick Brydone
to William Beckford, 1785.

# MARTIN COLE
# WINE DARK SEA

photoworks

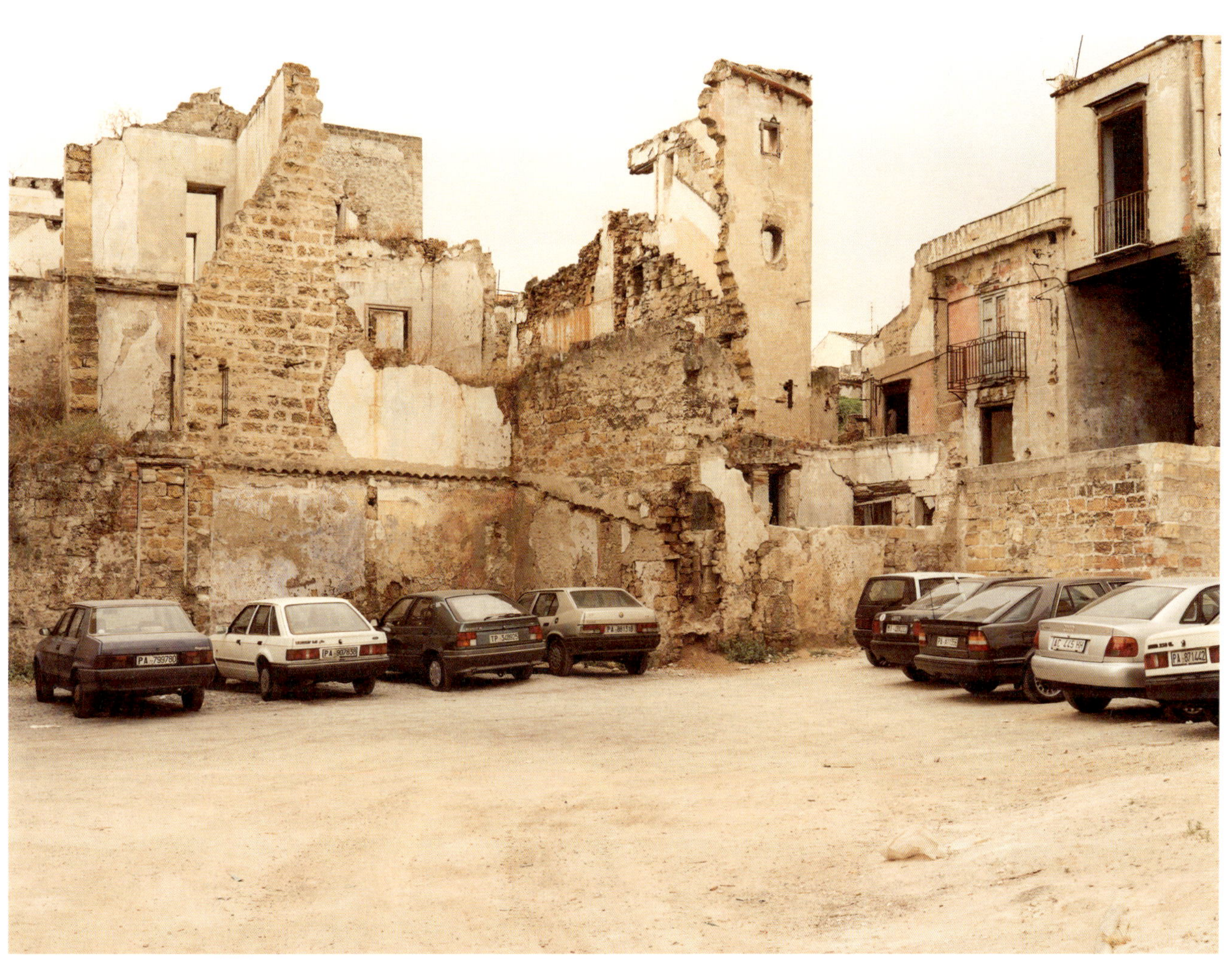

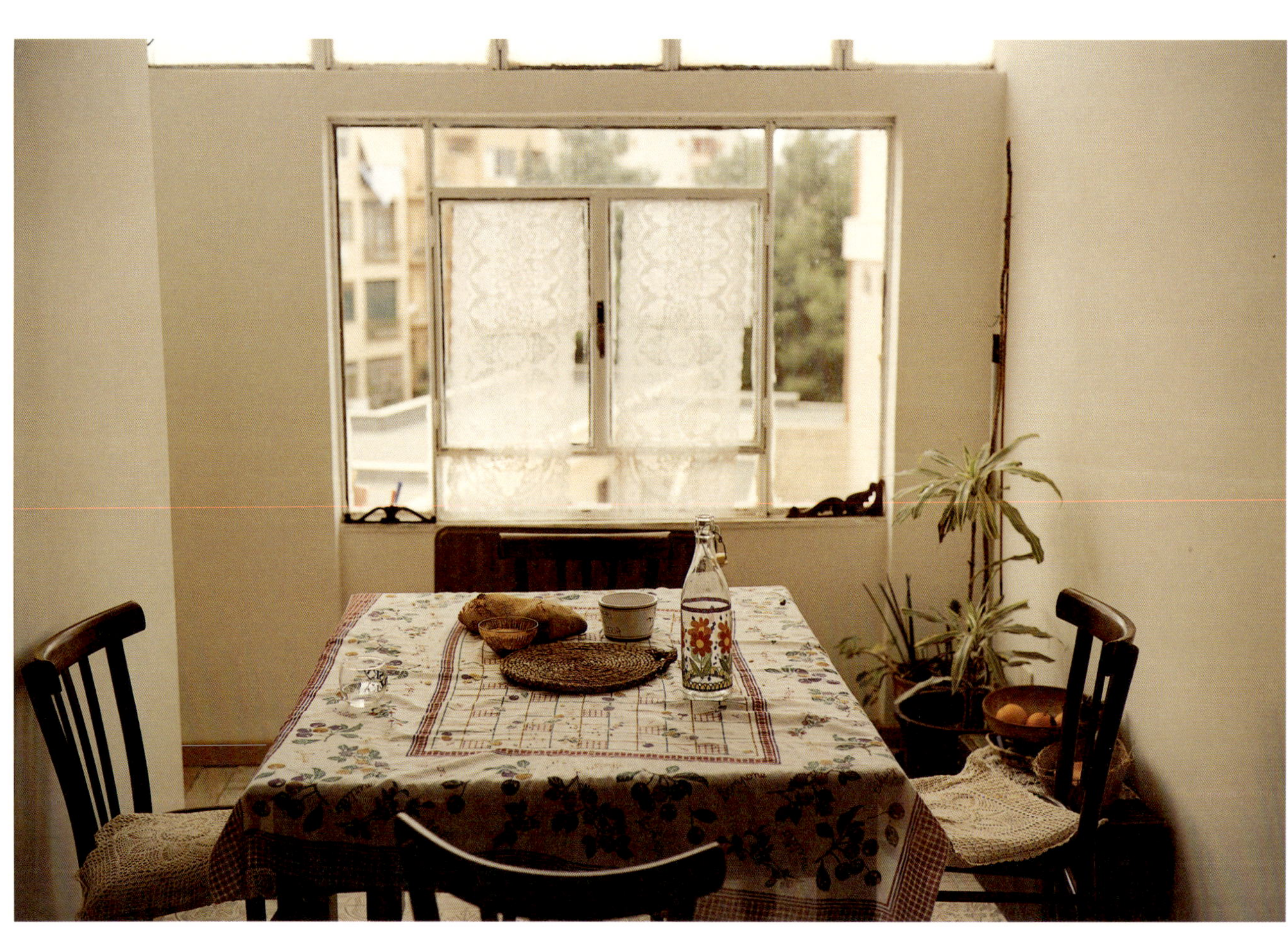

# Contents

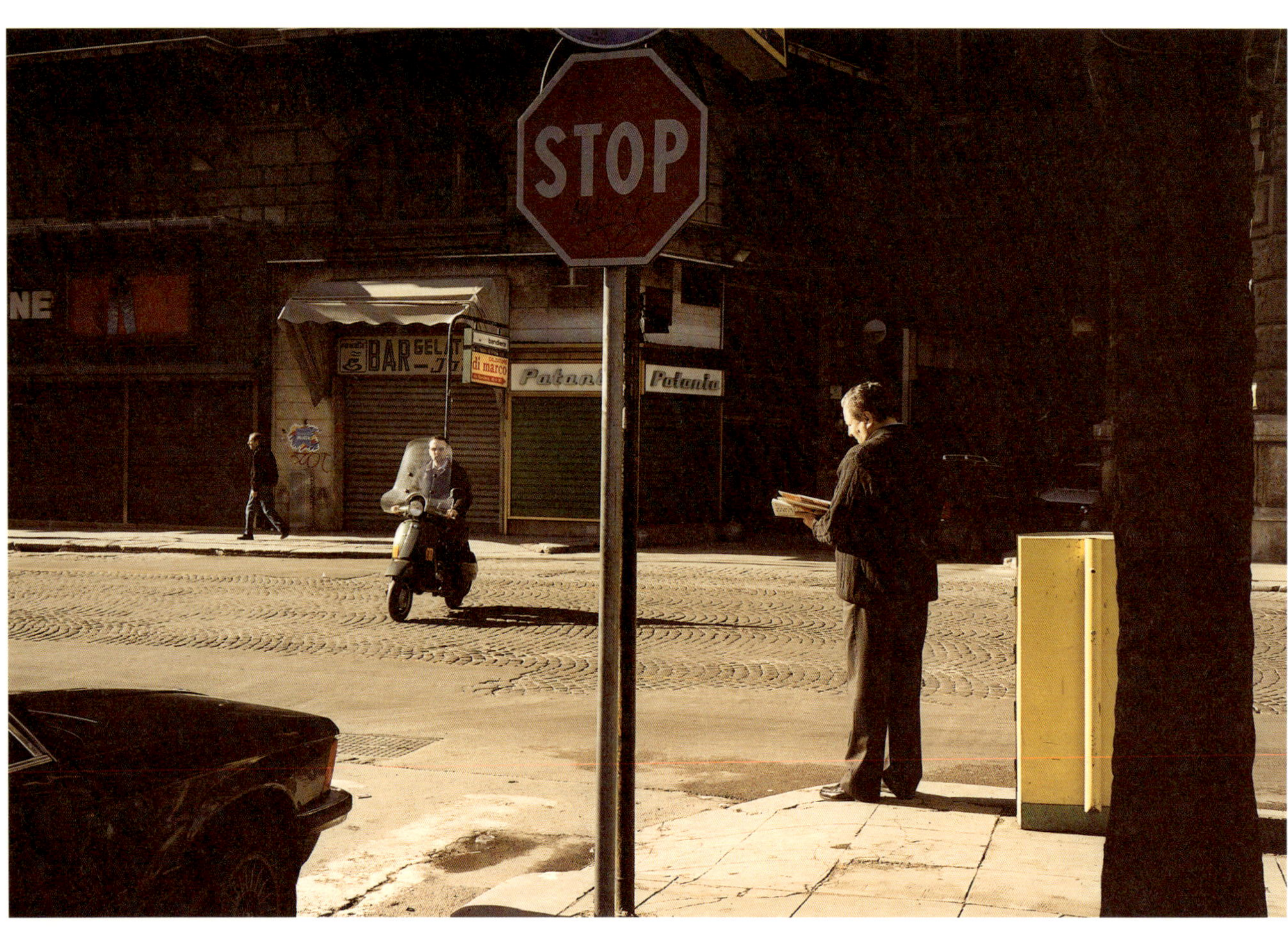
STOP
BAR
di marco

## Wine Dark Sea

Martin Cole

Wine and blood have a similar hue, and this was not lost to Homer, nor the heroes of his narratives who had a primal relationship with both. Homer described the Aegean as the 'wine dark sea', evoking a rich sense of threat through his metaphor, and underlining the sea's vital place in human life. The phrase has been used before in connection with Palermo; by Goethe, in his *Italian Journey*, and later by the Palermitan writer Leonardo Sciascia in his 1975 novel, *The Wine Dark Sea*. Palermo, unlike other European Mediterranean cities, faces north; behind it an encircling ring of high mountains. The Mediterranean Sea, normally so blue and light, is dark here, a brooding mixture of purples and blacks, and it is undeniably beautiful. But it is a sombre beauty, shot through with the anxiety of unknown depths.

I first visited Palermo in 1994. At that time, a new mayor, Leoluca Orlando, had been elected on a wave of public feeling against the Mafia and their hold over the lives of ordinary people. Orlando and a few others had begun the task of rebuilding the city's civic pride. There were large-scale anti-Mafia demonstrations that looked and felt like Eastern Europe. It was shocking to discover in Western Europe a place so sunk in tyranny. The rise to power of the Sicilian Mafia since World War II in the island, and to a great extent throughout the Italian mainland, is a well-documented story. The empty night-time streets (in a Mediterranean city) which constituted a de facto curfew, along with a particular kind of silence, reminded me strongly of 1980s Rumania. Both places appeared to me as looking-glass versions of our own society where the values we take for granted are inverted. The idea of truth in particular, whether societal or personal, seemed particularly problematic.

While Ceaucescu lived out the last years of his reign, a battle was being fought through the streets of Palermo as three families struggled for control of the heroin distribution in Europe and North America. During that decade the official death toll ran into the thousands in what the writer Alexander Stille described as: 'Palermo's descent into the long night of one of the most bloody and tragic periods any European city has known since World War II.' The dead included many public servants – lawyers, policemen, judges and members of parliament, journalists and soldiers – anyone who stood in the way of the 'men of honour'. Tanks stood on street corners, in a vain attempt to represent the authority of the state.

By 1988, a certain Judge Falcone had managed to break through the silence surrounding the bosses, and some three hundred top Mafia men stood trial in Palermo. A special underground bunker was built for the occasion, as the CIA and the Italian State joined forces to break the Mafia. It was the first time that anybody (despite the evidence) had publicly admitted the existence of a secret society, and for Sicilians it was a traumatic and historic period.

The State ultimately won the battle, but lost the war. Three years later only a handful of those indicted were still in jail. Italy's greatest post-war statesman, and seven times Prime Minister, Giulio Andreoti was facing trial for conspiracy to murder. The Mafia was buying up the Italian state piece by piece, and offering the world a new economic model, one of ruthless corporate capitalism unfettered by any laws, and capable of supplanting the state.

Heidelberg-educated, and a self-professed fan of Voltaire, Mayor Orlando fought the Mafia with cultural as well as political weapons.

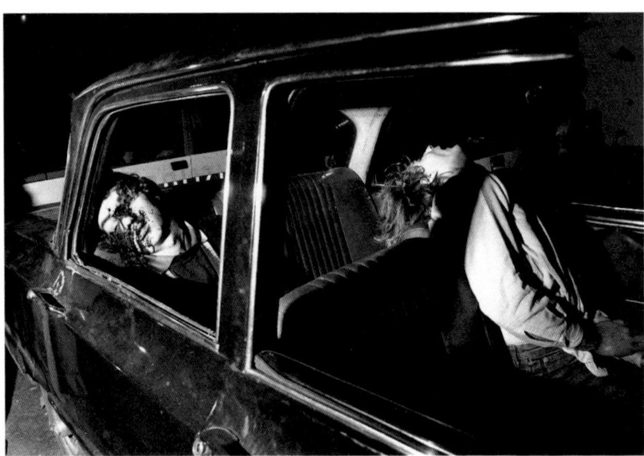

Franco Zecchin
Double homicide in the Zen district, Palermo, 30 march 1981.

In addition to blocking new developments and beginning restoration work on the old city, he launched countless cultural initiatives aimed at linking Palermo to the rest of Europe. Numerous 'events' were staged, musical, theatrical, and cinematic, all at night and outdoors, trying to bring people out of their houses to reclaim their city. When McDonalds opened a branch in Palermo, Orlando and those of like mind were thrilled at this symbol of connectedness, this ambassador of normality.

A program was initiated to open buildings of historic interest to the public, as is the case in other European cities. Palermo is one of the world's great baroque masterpieces. In 1996 the administration opened the Scirocco Rooms of a well known Palazzo. We went there on a hot August day and, descending a spiral staircase set in the main courtyard, we dropped down from the brilliant white of noon into a vast series of man made caves. Wooden walkways traversed what appeared to be an underground lake. This had once been a well dug out by the Arabs. The air was wonderfully cool, but there was something of the crypt about it also. I tried to imagine the noble family decamping to these cool chambers with their retinue of servants, fleeing from the hot Saharan wind and forced underground in a perverse hibernation.

Two years later, finding ourselves in the vicinity, we decided to revisit the Scirocco Room. The same caretaker was in his little booth in the courtyard. The Scirocco Room, however, was closed, as was the rest of the palace. He explained sorrowfully that the money for projects of this kind had gone. Jobs had been cut, buildings closed down. This was a familiar, sad story. Rumours circulated that all available monies had gone into Orlando's re-election fund.

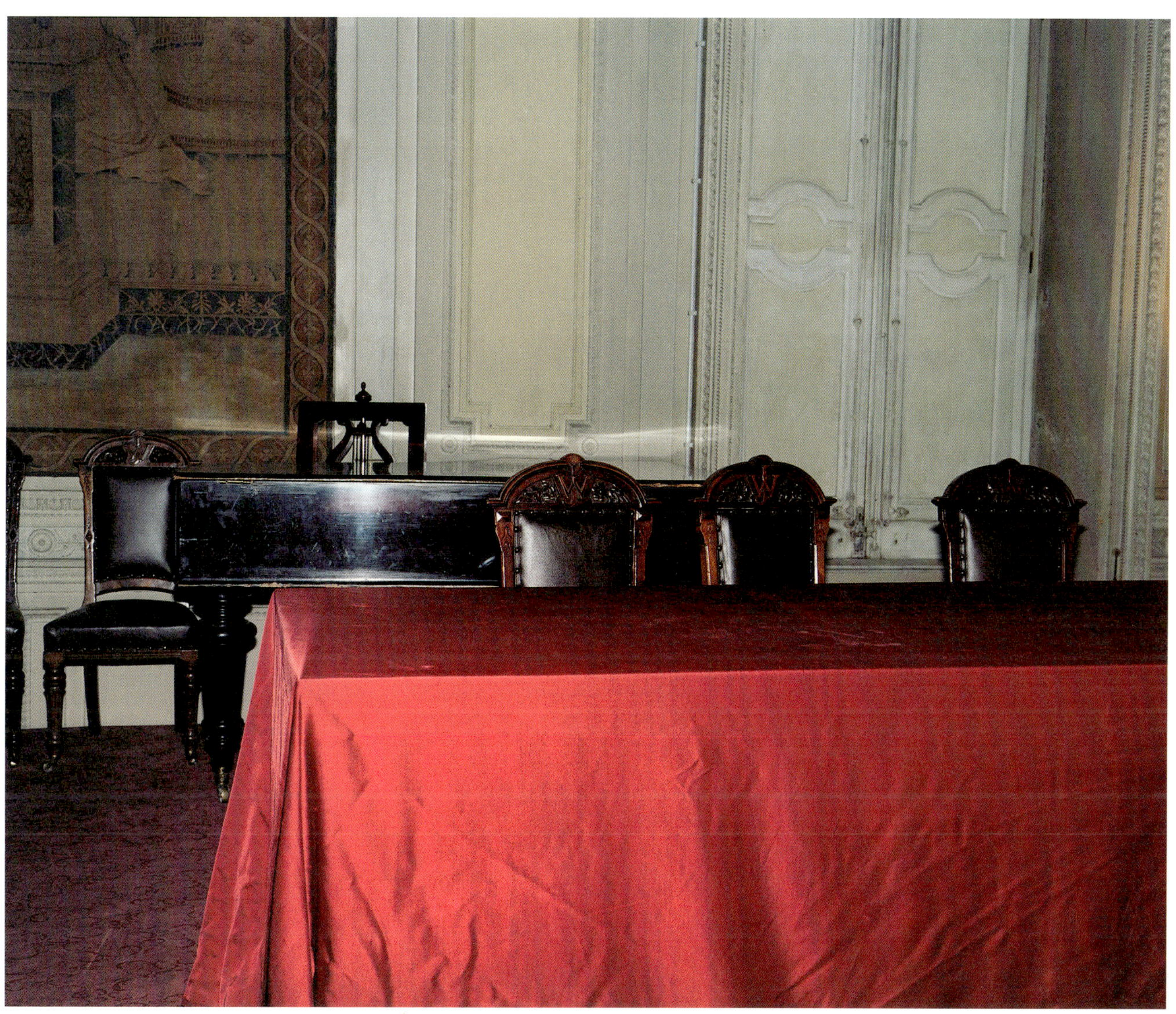

2

Before I started making photographs in Sicily I looked around for previous work, paintings or photographs – a visual reference point that might help me to frame my own observations. My practice up to this point had been concerned with landscape and its representation, so it was natural that I should want to look at landscape images of Sicily. I found very few. There was a lot of homegrown photography in the style of Cartier Bresson, some of it very good, and in its own way unique. In particular, the photographers Letizia Battaglia and Franco Zecchin with their haunting images of murder victims. Taken for the daily paper *L'ora*, they were a political gesture, showing people on a daily basis the corpses they so wanted to forget, and they appeared to me as a bald and explicit meditation on death itself.

Historically, there was no shortage of pictures of the islanders themselves, *i siciliani,* a cast of thousands, a massive index of faces and figures fixed forever in black and white, enacting a million decisive moments by the sea, in the fields, the slums and the palaces – always under the tyranny of the southern sun. Renato Guttoso the most famous of Sicilian (and Italian) realist painters rarely showed an unpopulated landscape, and his giant vivid canvasses are full of a carnal humanity, a Sicilian realism of the flesh.

In the winter of 1995, I came across an exhibition at the botanical gardens entitled *Les Voyageurs Sicilian.* This show brought together the writings and lithographs of foreign travellers to Sicily during the last years of the eighteenth century: Northern European travellers indulging in *grand tourism.* Looking through the catalogue to the exhibition I was quite surprised by the essays written by contemporary academics from the University of Palermo. I had always

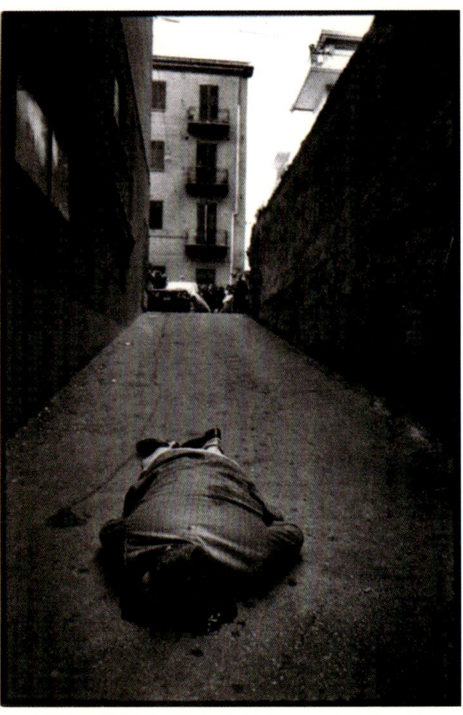

Letizia Battaglia,
Body of Giuseppe lo Bardo,
Palermo, 7 march 1977.

imagined that Italians of the south must have felt patronised at best by these bustling know-it-alls from up north, 'discovering' their heritage and telling them all about it. In fact there seemed to be a universal consensus that these men were saviours of a unique heritage. Tireless excavators (the discipline of modern archaeology was born in southern Italy at this time, principally through Winkleman), and classifiers, they saved and preserved for a grateful posterity the remains of Magnae Grecia. In so doing, they brought with them the ideas of the Enlightenment, helping to link Sicily to modern Europe. Sicily was not on the menu for the average grand tour, its isolation both physical and cultural was legendary; it suffered from earthquakes and eruptions, and was full of bandits and dangerous wild animals; it had a strange language, extreme climate, and bizarre manners. On the other hand, the rewards for the intrepid traveller were great. Sicily was the greater part of Magnae Grecia, and Syracuse, Agrigento, Segesta, Sellinunte, were some of the greatest cities of the Hellenistic era. These were the best ruins outside of Greece, all in need of classification and excavation. In the age of Romanticism, there was also the rumour that in Sicily, the old gods had never really died.

Of literary accounts of journeys to Sicily at this time, none is more justly famous than Goethe's chapter on Sicily in his *Italian Journey*. Sicily, he confidently asserts, is the key to understanding Italy itself. He expects, eccentrically, to find there his 'archetypal plant form', the existence of which occurred to him six months previously in the botanical gardens at Verona. In Sicily Goethe finds a cultural and natural endgame to his Italian adventure, as he broods over ancient ruins and primal volcanic geology.

Reading through these various accounts from the dawn of the modern age, I was interested to note what I might have in common with these travellers. On the face of it not much – their lofty ambitions and sense of purpose together with a certain arrogance, spoke of a different era. Their was *something*, though, which had to do with their *Northerness*, a sense of what it is to be programmed by climate and geography and culture, and through travelling, to subtly tamper with that programming.

It was also interesting to speculate about what had changed and what remained the same over a given time and in a specific landscape. Looking at a landscape in this way, conventional notions of historical periods that 'succeed' each other seem inadequate. Instead, one era superimposes itself onto another without totally obscuring it. Physically this is nowhere more apparent than in Sicily. In my mind (if nowhere else) the Romanticism of the late eighteenth century still exists like a ghostly image imprinted on the landscape, underneath or alongside the evidence of the social upheavals, wars, and construction of the ensuing two centuries.

With these ideas in mind I began photographing a sequence of topographical views of the city from various vantage points in the surrounding mountains. This was a kind of psychological map making. Having been immersed in the city (where even the locals have problems knowing which road leads where, as if their forgetfulness of the physical layout of the city somehow mirrored a more fundamental malaise), it was a wonderful illusion to see the city in its entirety, a solvable riddle. Yet over time, the project broke the bounds of this initial concern. Finally the photographs divided themselves into three distinct but interrelated series: Firstly, photographs of the city and the coastal plain on which it is situated; secondly, the mountains and the interior, and lastly, a rocky cape to the northwest of the city.

Fernand Braudel in his seminal work, *A History of the Mediterranean and the Mediterranean World in the Age of Phillip II,* talks of the archetypal Mediterranean city. It lies facing the sea on the fertile coastal littoral. Behind it are the mountains. To settle the coastal strip required an advanced civilisation, powerful enough to ward off attacks. Over the centuries bands of refugees or nomadic peoples arriving at this fertile plain, but without the means to exploit or hold it, would retreat to the high mountains where they could eke out a meagre living with a few goats or sheep, relatively safe from aggressors, yet stuck in a life that was harsh and unchanging. The fertile littoral around Palermo has hosted successive civilisations from the Phoenicians, Greeks, Romans and Arabs through to the Normans and their modern descendents. The mountains behind are scantily populated and have historically offered only a relatively primitive existence. It could be argued that over the last couple of centuries the life of Palermo has been disproportionately influenced by the clannish, ruthless and primitive values of the mountains. Some historians see the origins of the Mafia in the brutal social structures engendered by life in these inhospitable locations. A friend of mine who had spent a year living in Sarajevo as a foreign correspondent once explained to me that behind the political divides lay other more ancient grievances, in particular the hatred of the mountain peasants for the cosmopolitan city dwellers. It was these mountain men she insisted, who, drunk, and from the safety of their mountain fastnesses, operated the guns that shelled the city below, giving vent to an atavistic jealously.

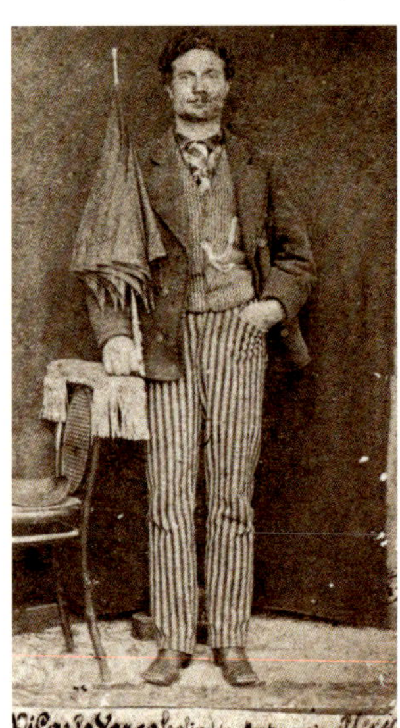

Anonymous portrait of the bandit Paolino di Carlo Varco, 1874.
Opposite:
M.Brocato. Portrait of the bandit Mauro Ortolani, 1894.

The Sicilian interior, where it is not mountainous, is given over to the production of wheat. In the ancient Greek pantheon, Sicily was the home of Demeter, goddess of the corn – and also according to this mythology, it is here that the plough was invented. The giant fields that roll for miles have for millennia been worked by peasants who would live huddled together for protection in hilltop towns. Often they would walk upwards of ten miles to their workplace in the early dawn. This system, which continued well into the twentieth century, was little more than slavery. The vast estates, or *latifunda* on which these people toiled were among the largest in Europe, and the great noble families who owned them lived elsewhere, in Palermo, mainland Italy, Madrid, Barcelona, or even London.

The last photographs depict Capo Gallo, a nature reserve that comprises the northwest cape of the bay of Palermo. Here the landscape speaks more of geological rather than historical time. The thousand-metre rocky bluff falls precipitously into the dark Mediterranean, creating a coastline of jagged rocks, underwater caves and abyssal drops. The only signs of human involvement here are recent, a few holiday villas, some World War II-era gun emplacements, and a fair amount of rubbish. Couples come here in cars and on motorbikes, leaving behind them condoms, cigarette butts and needles.

In Sicily, one encounters a European landscape that is neither post-industrial nor postmodern; here is a landscape in many respects unchanged for a thousand years. The author Norman Lewis writes about the plain of Partinico on the outskirts of Palermo, that the settlement pattern has remained the same since Roman

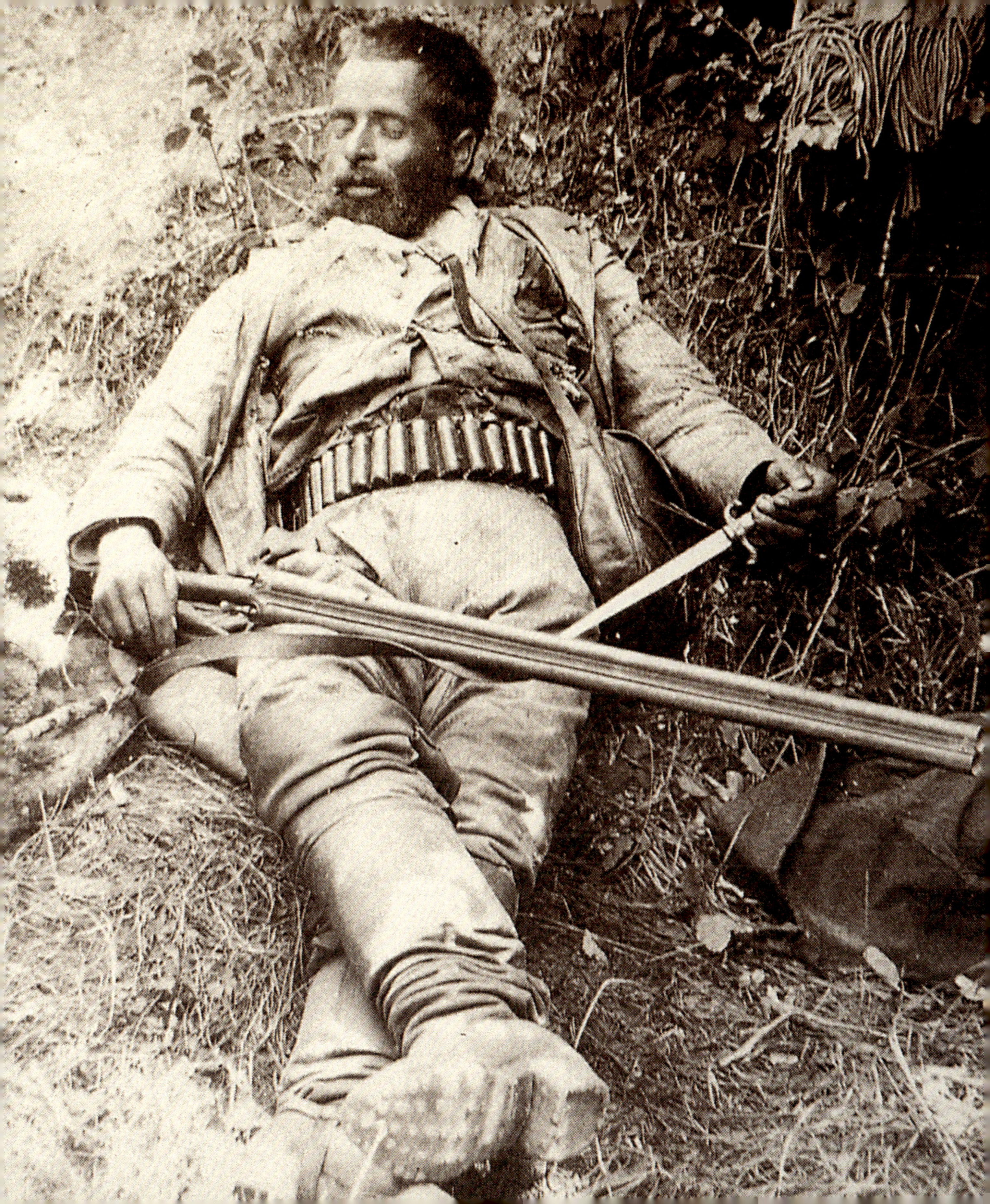

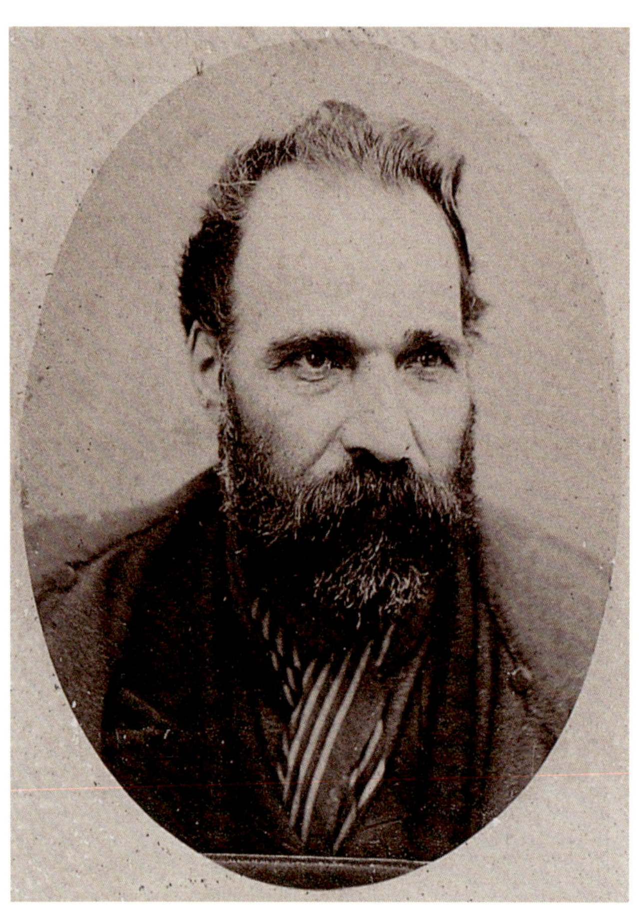

Anonymous portrait of the Mafioso
Michelle Amoroso, 1885

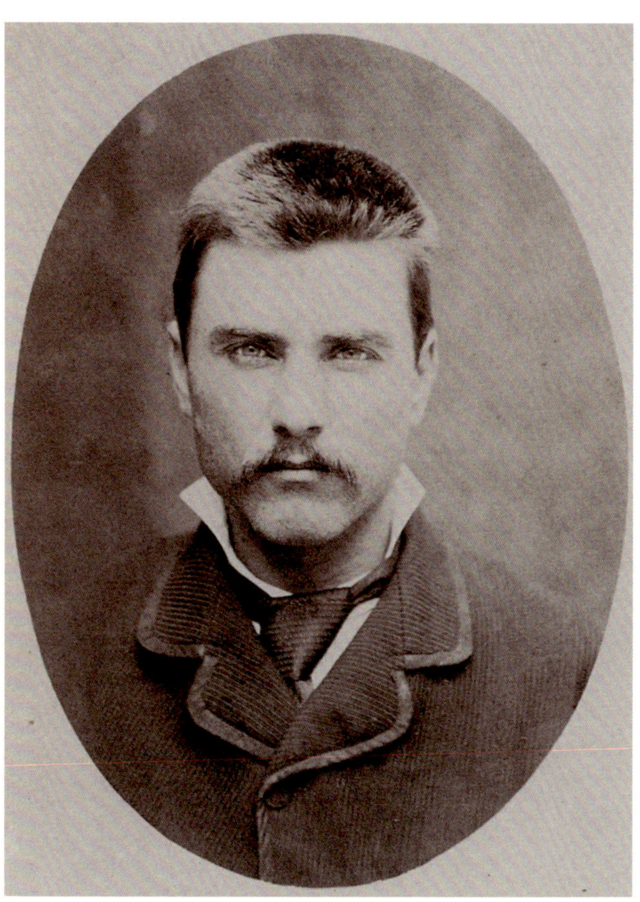

Anonymous portrait of the Mafioso
Carmelo Mendola, 1885.

times, and that from the hills behind you can see a perfect simulacrum of an antique landscape. This unchanged aspect of much of the countryside, in any other European country, would be something to exploit, a selling point: Tudor cottages, old castles, Roman roads, picturesque, quaint, and with only the most benign of connections to the present. In Sicily, this is not the case. In spite of the best efforts of the government to encourage tourism, and exploit their vast warehouse of historical sites and treasures, the Sicilian landscape in the main is one that resists the demands of consumerism and access in a negative fashion. No one walks, cycles, camps, picnics or lives in it. It is an expression of power relationships that elsewhere in Europe disappeared after the industrial revolution.

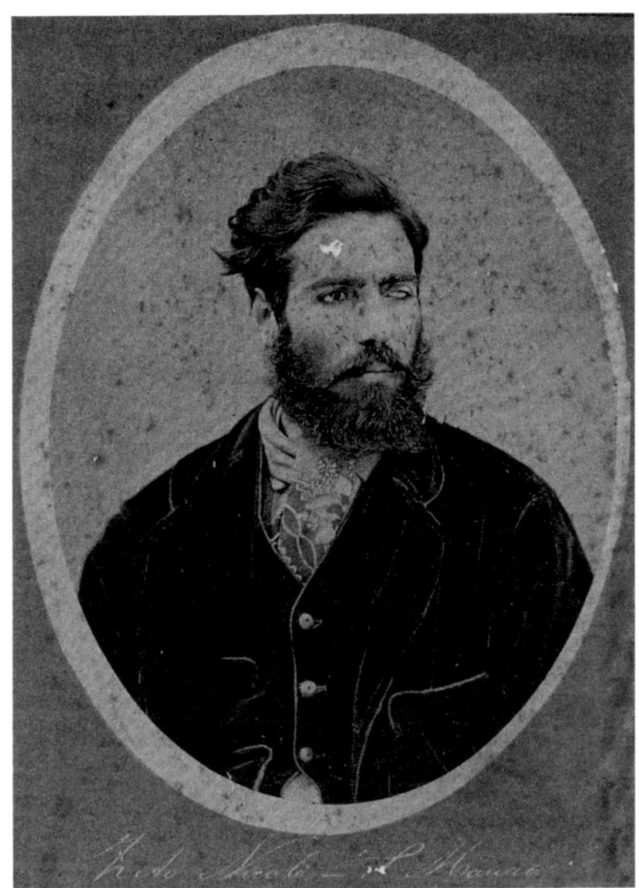

Enrico Seffer portrait of the bandit
Nicolo Zito, 1877

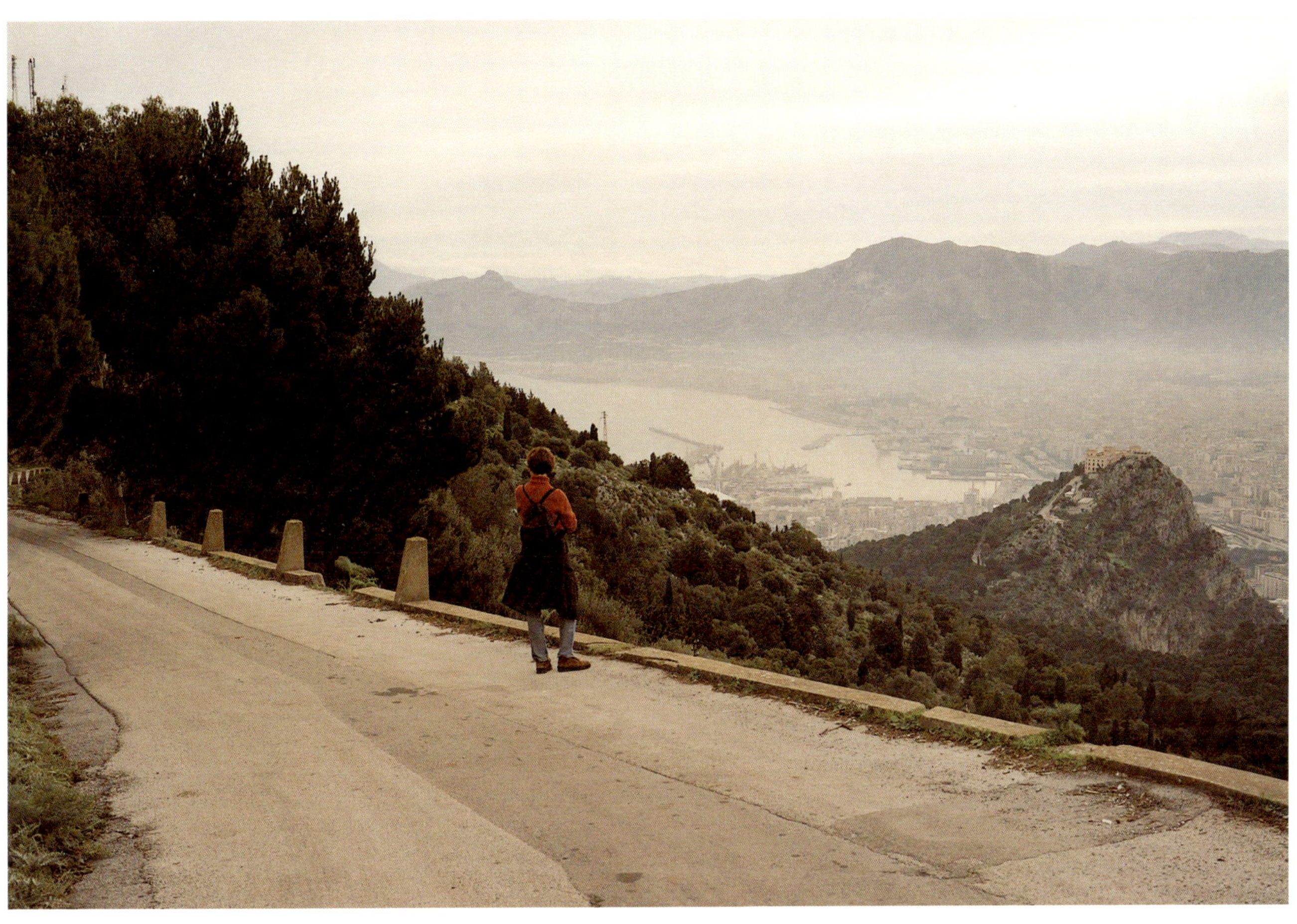

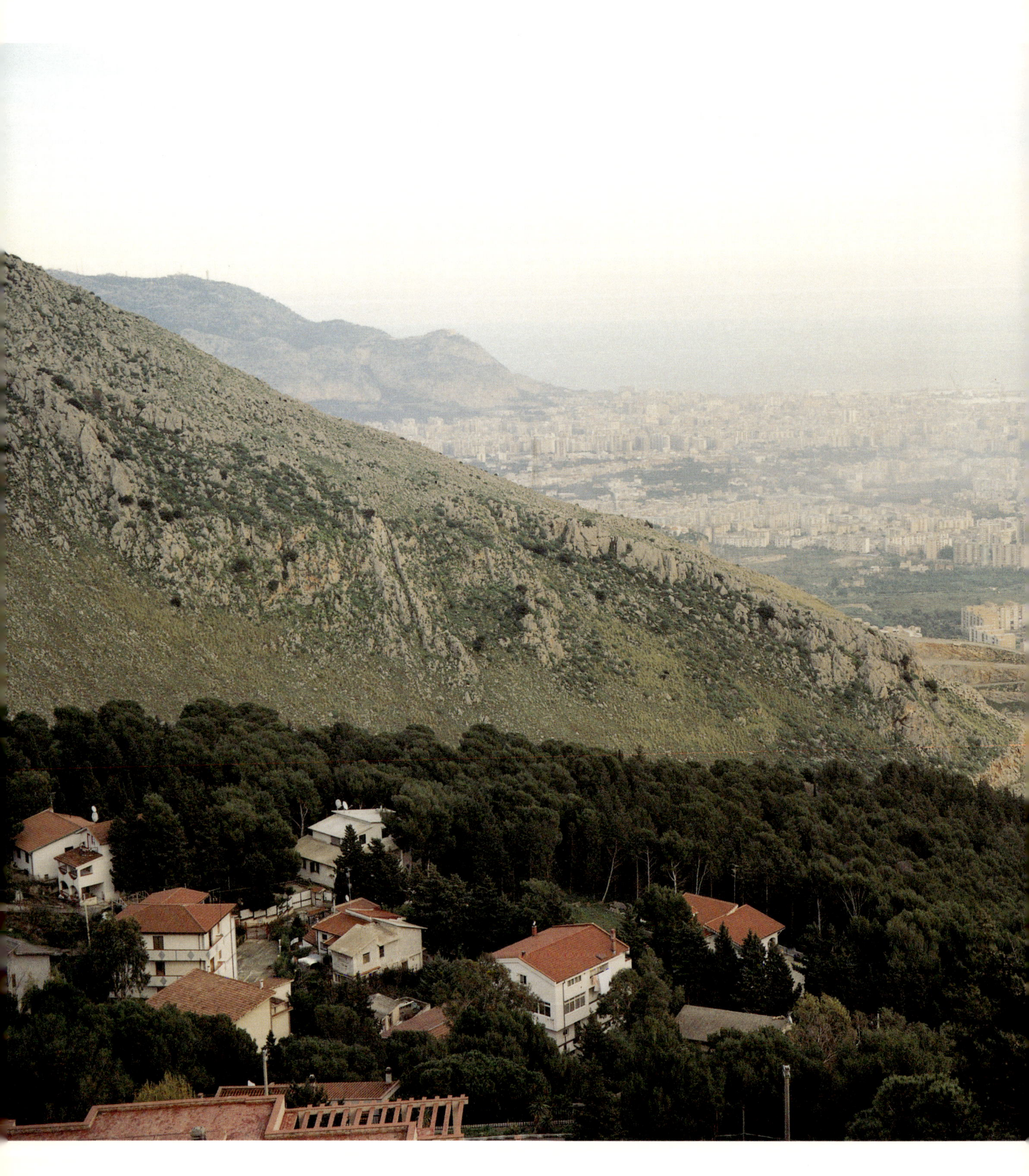

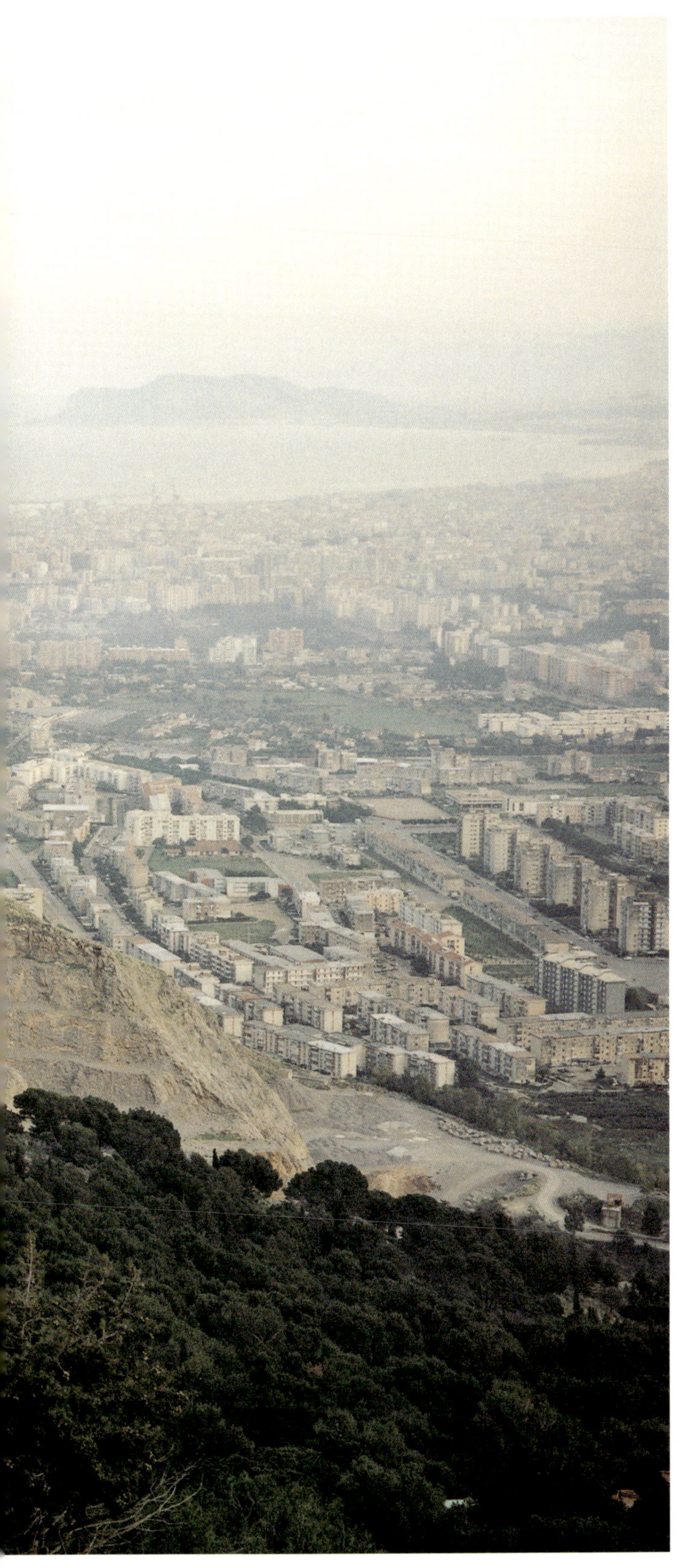

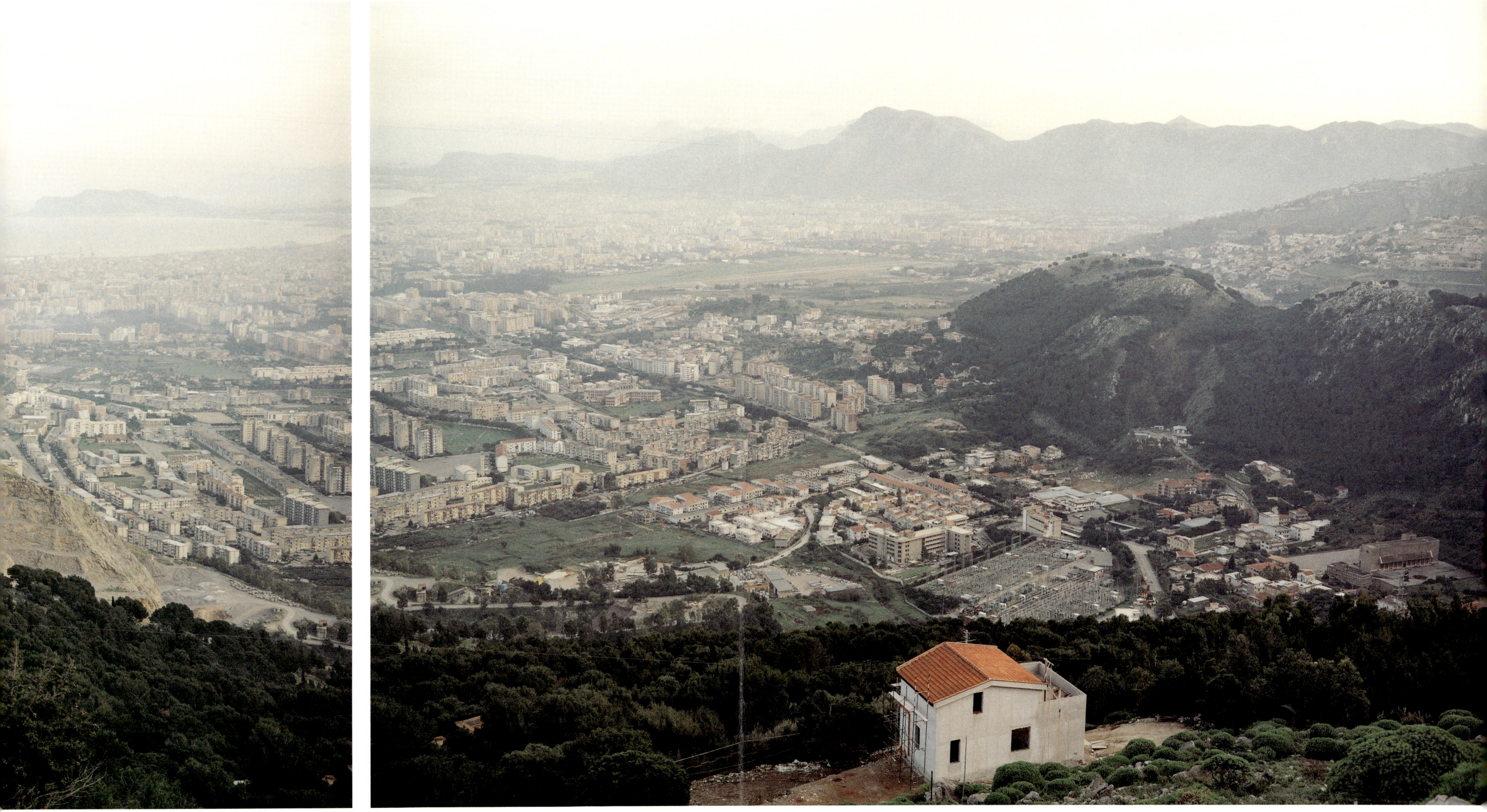

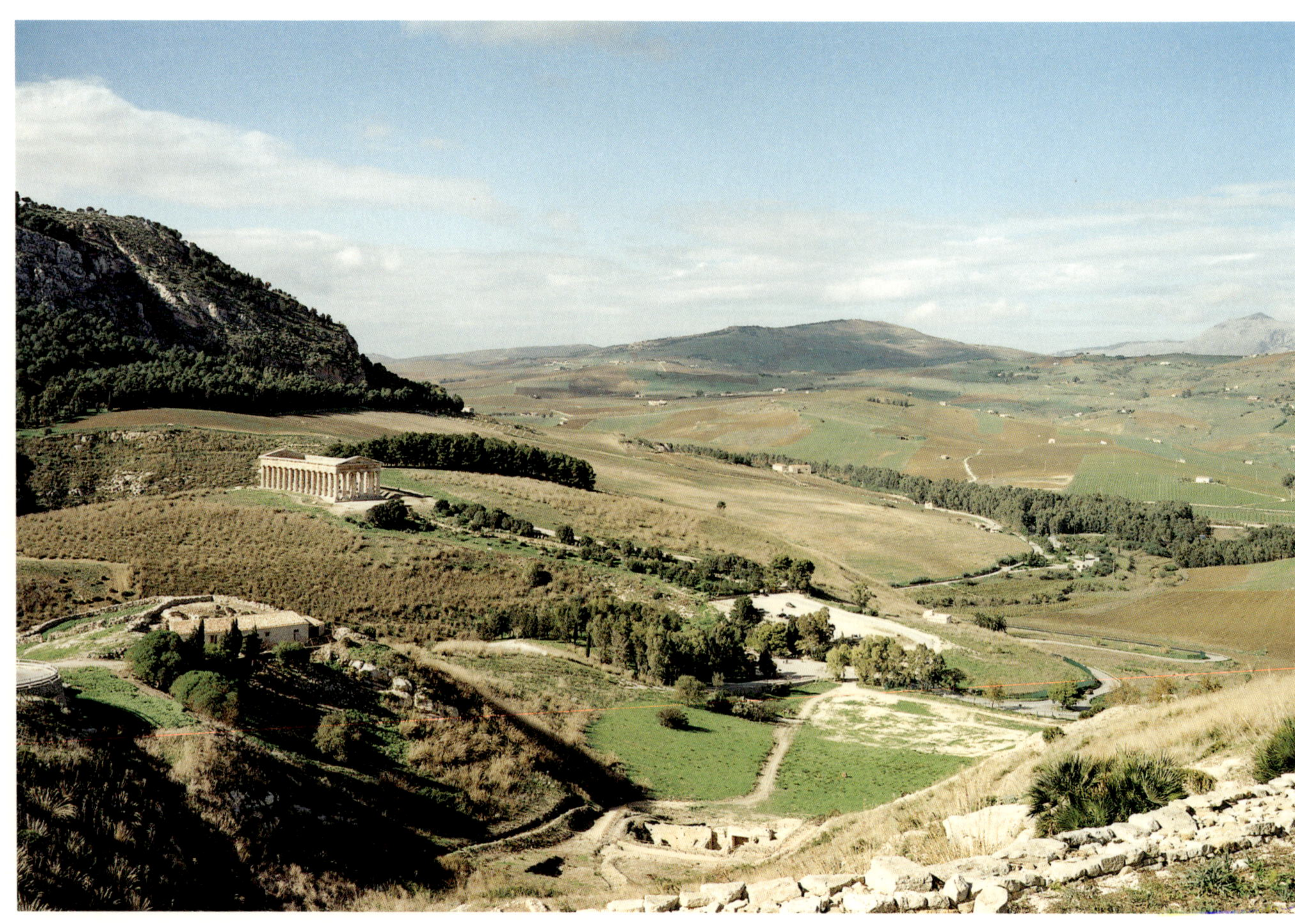

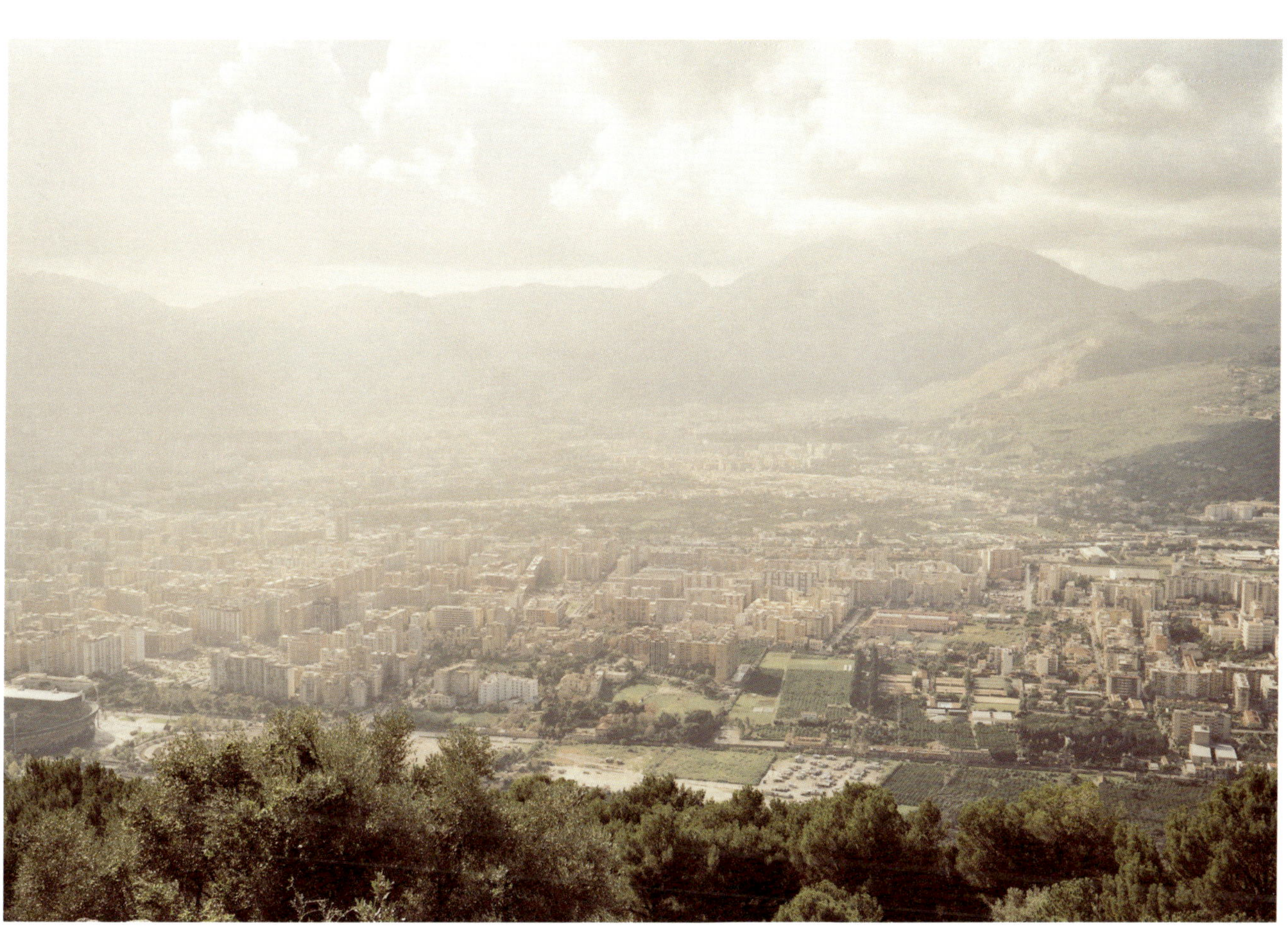

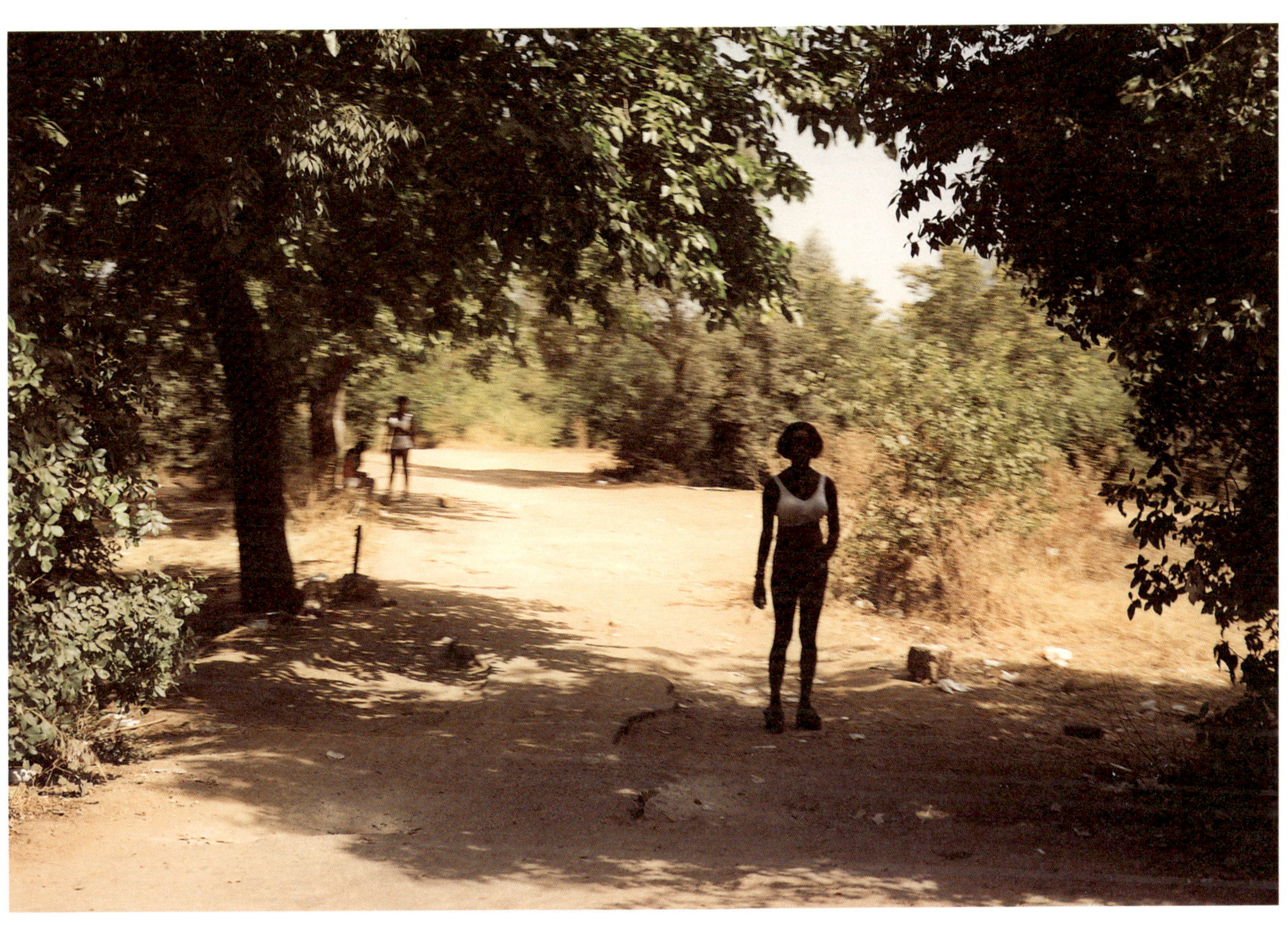

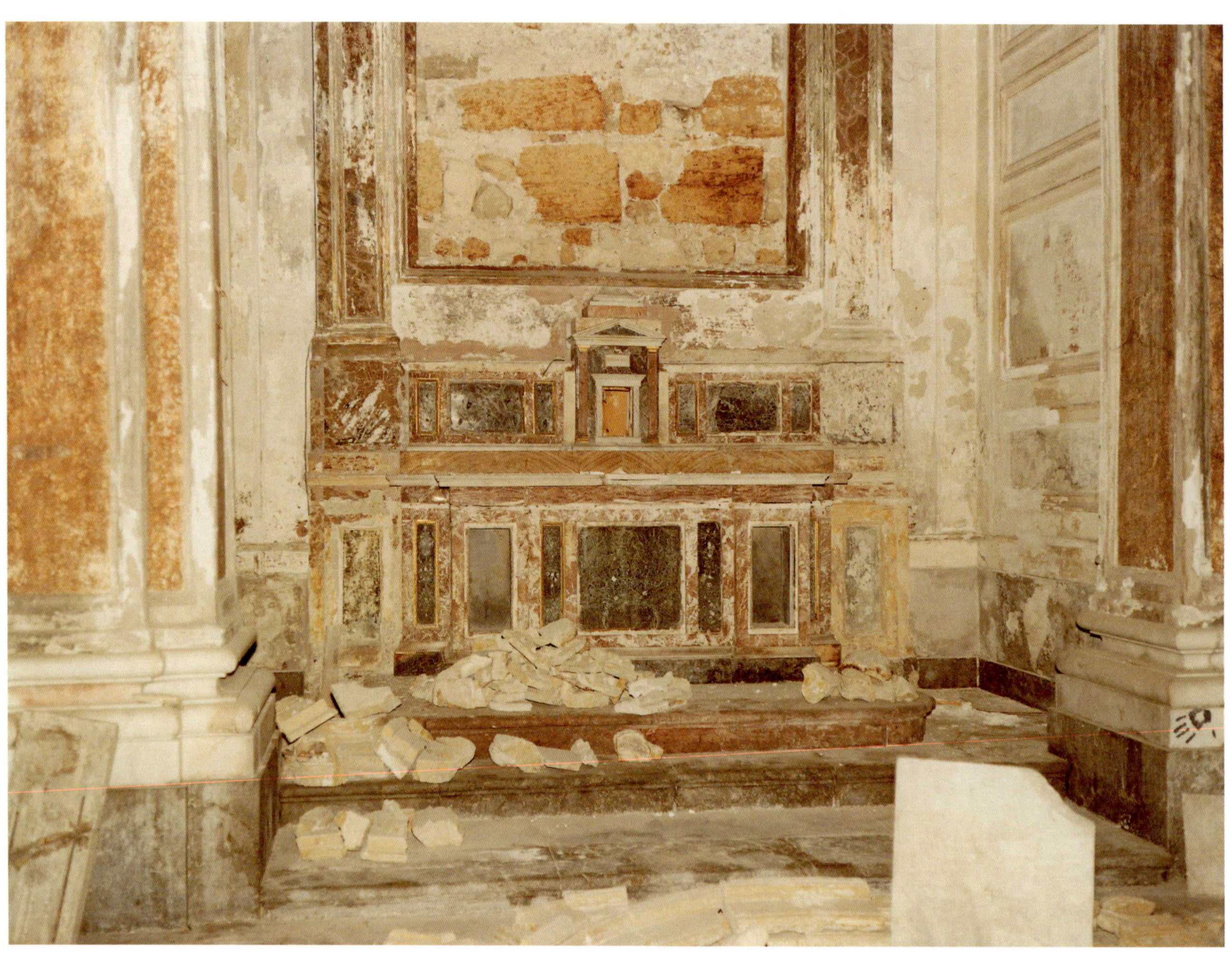

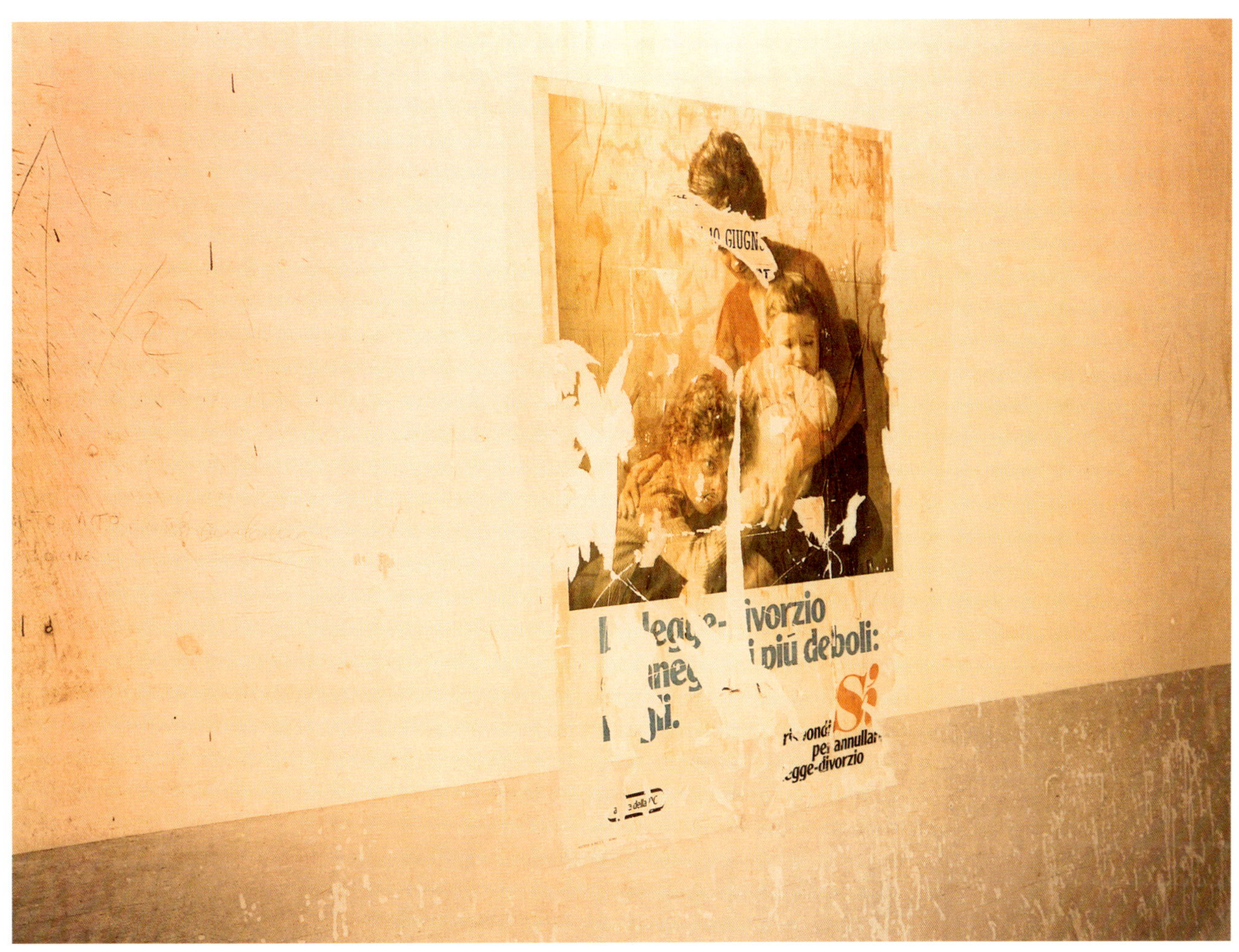

GIUGN
ivorzio
più deboli:
per annullar
egge-divorzio

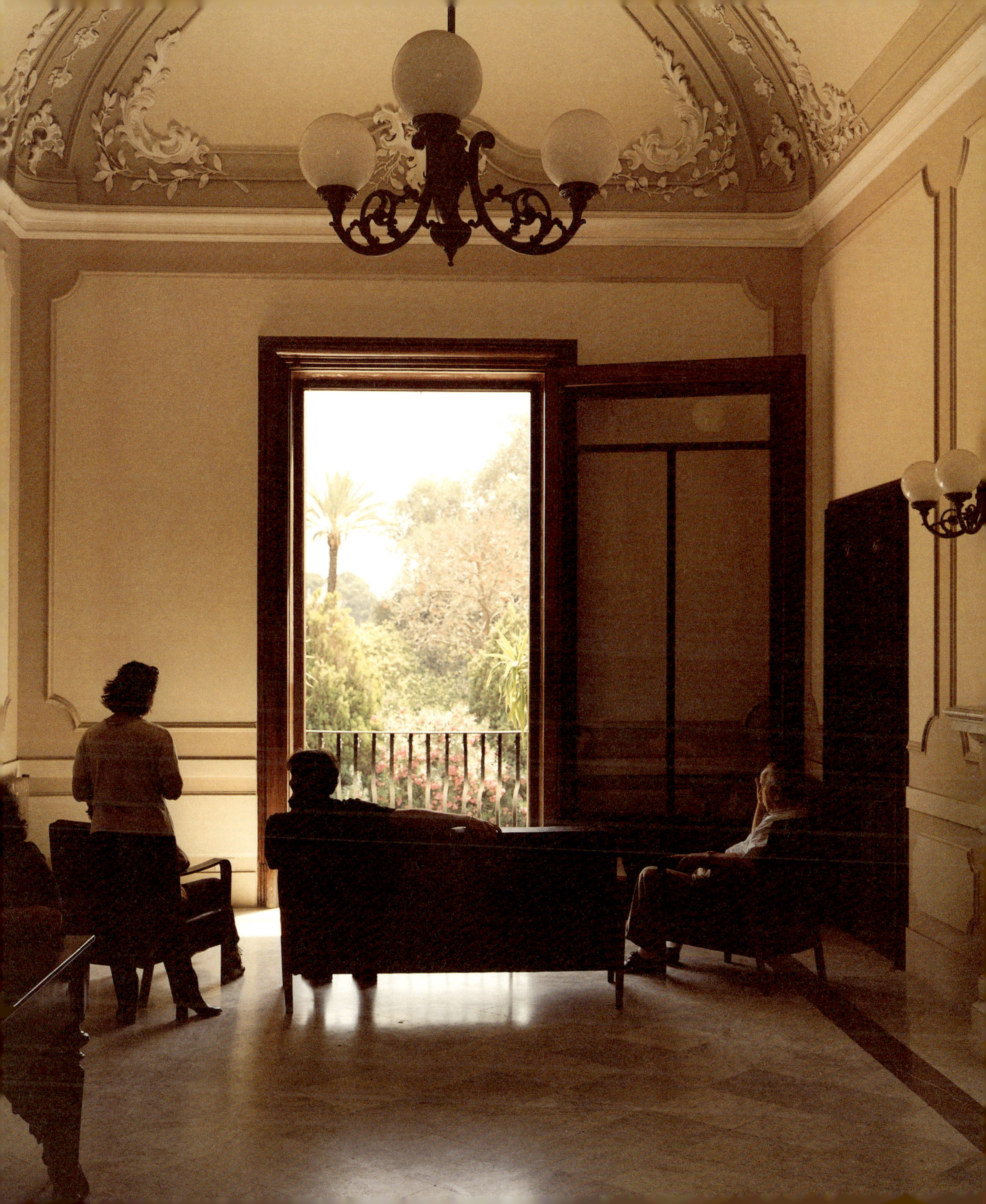

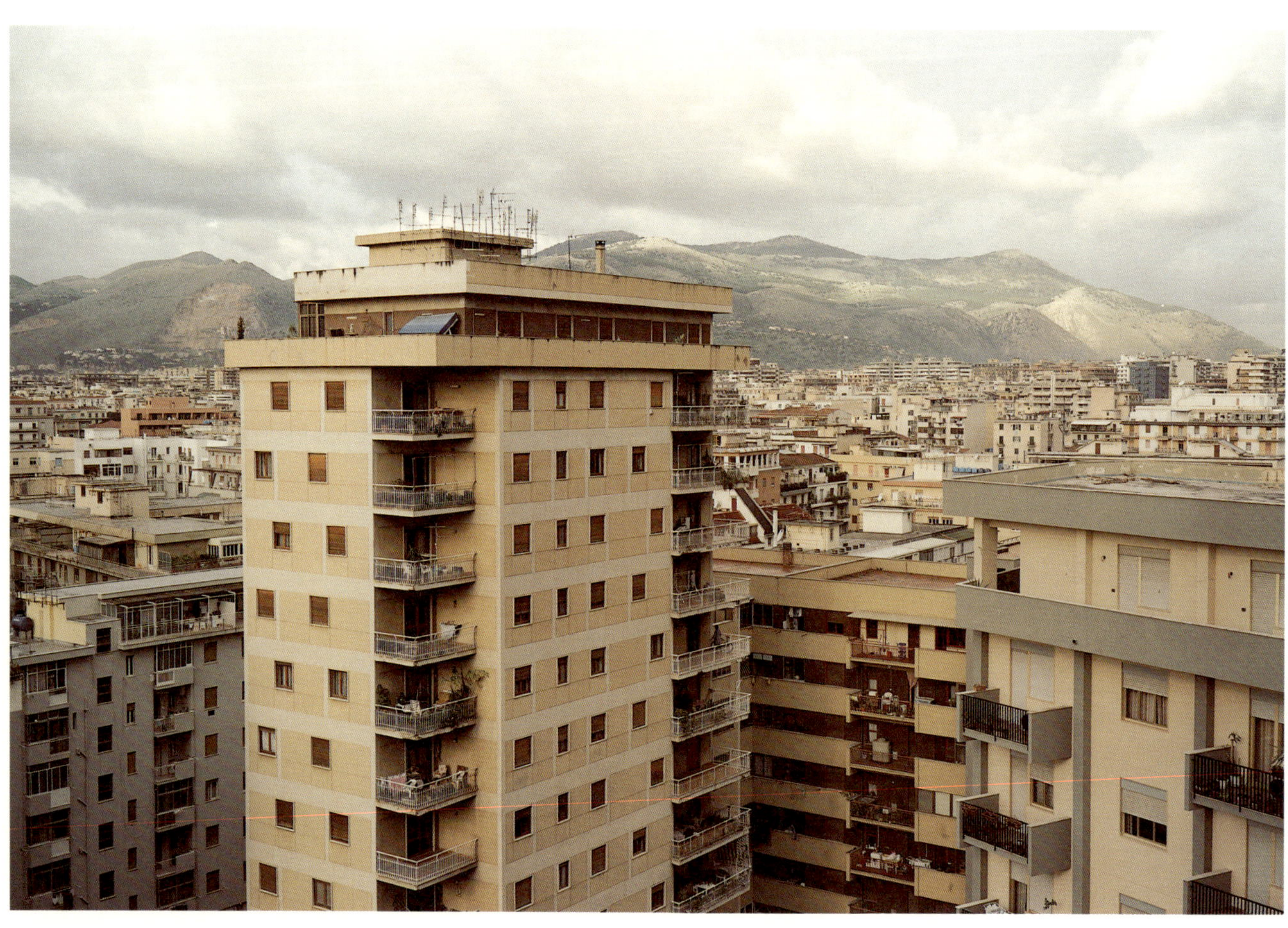

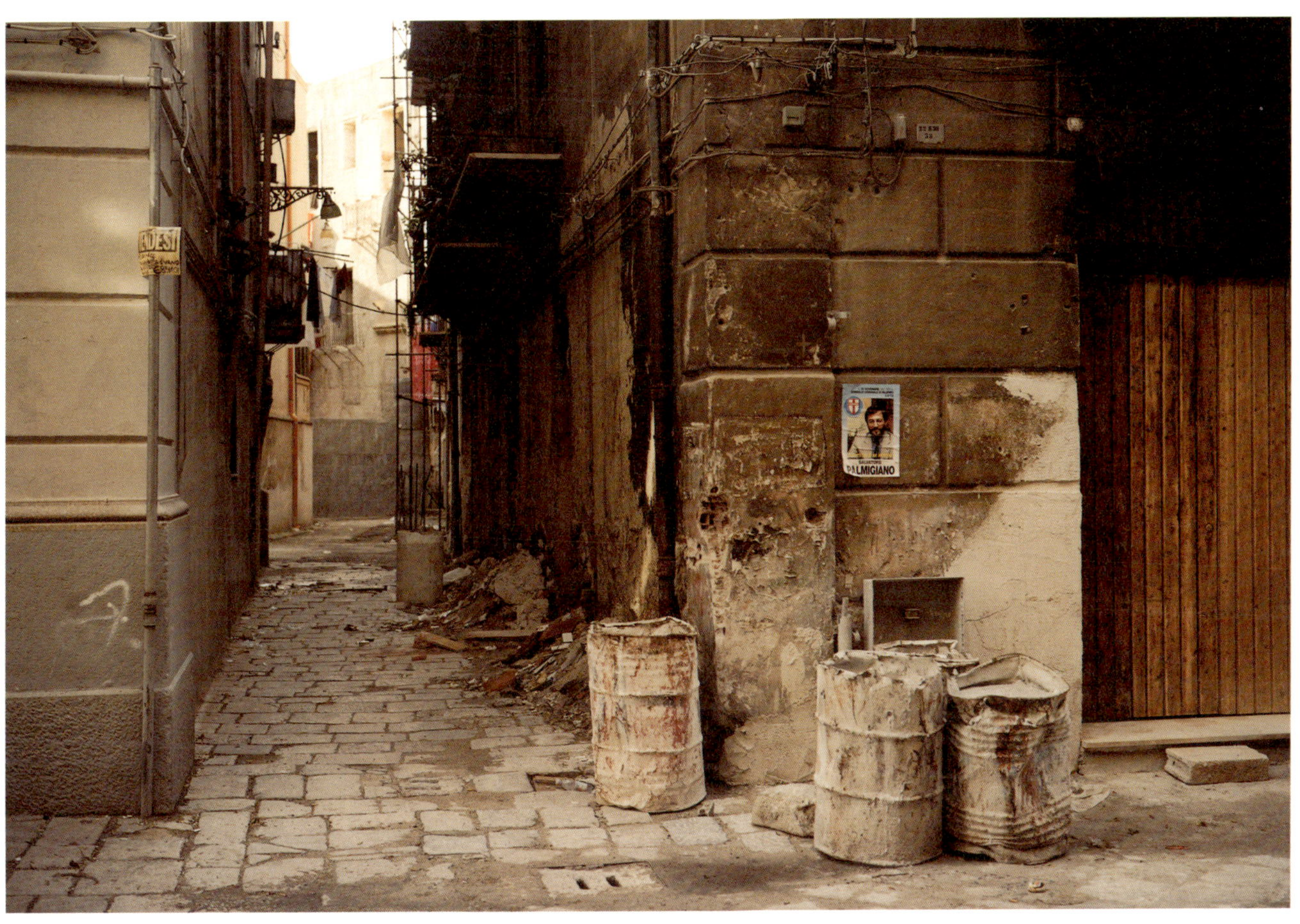
PALMIGIANO

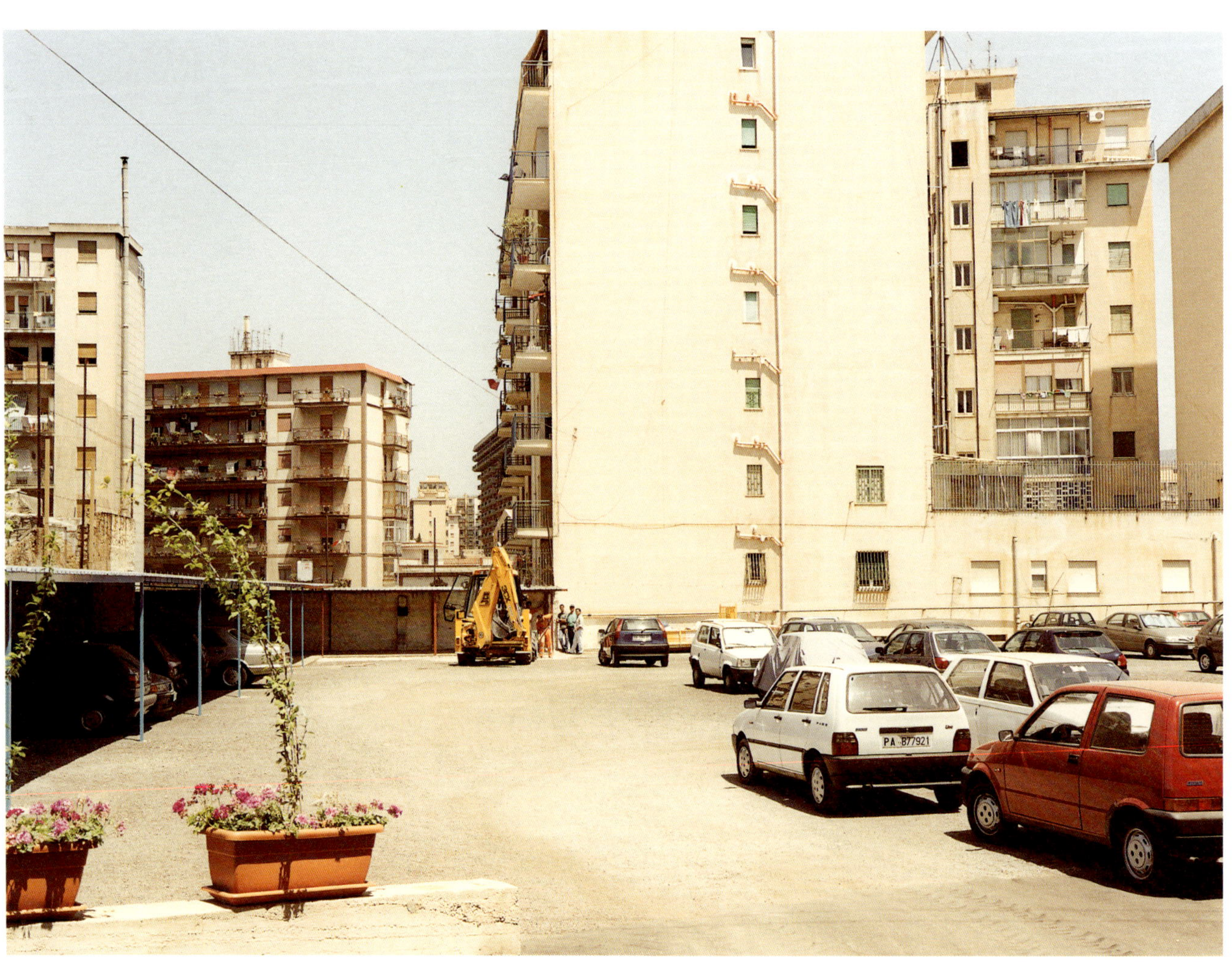
PA B77921

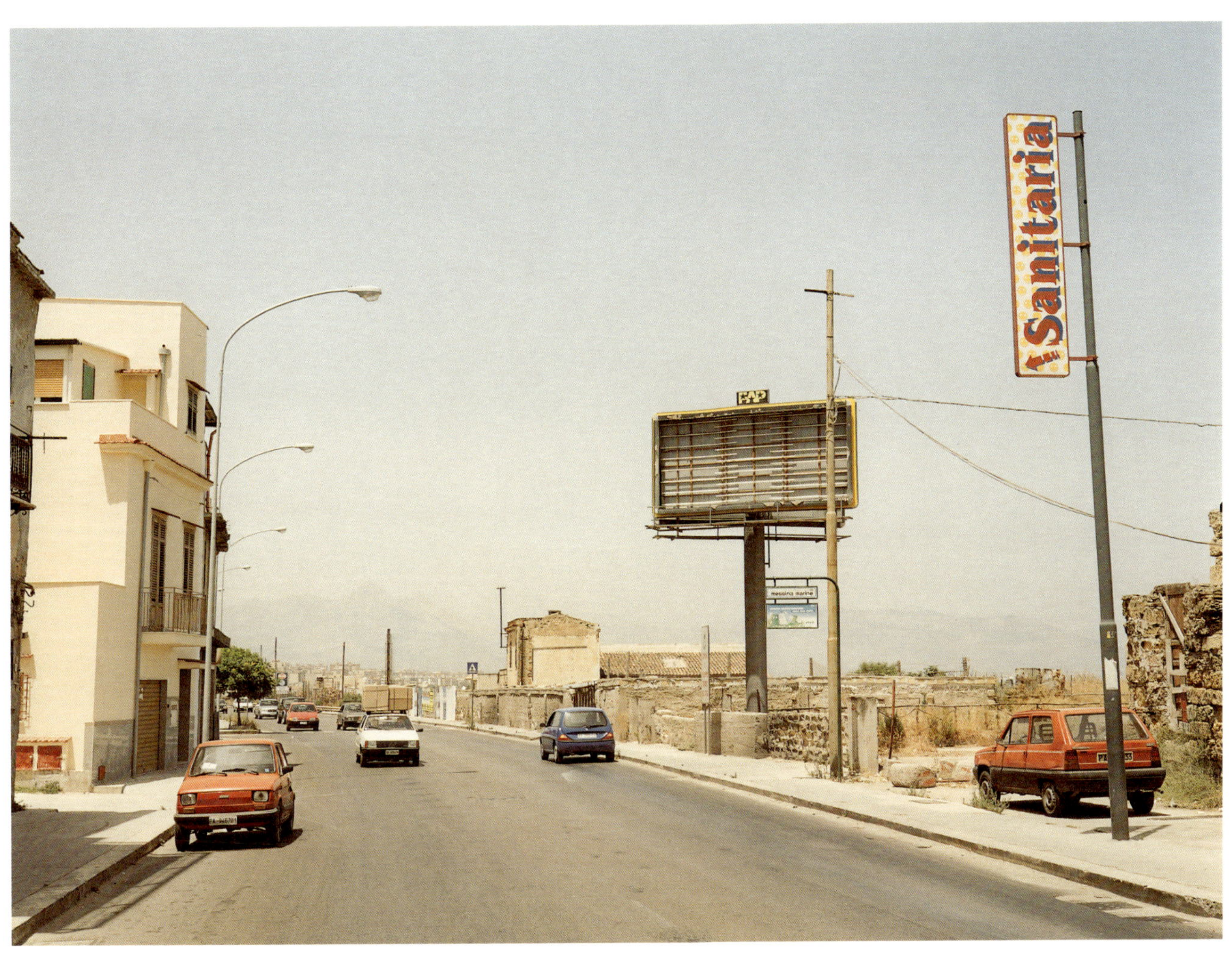
Sanitaria

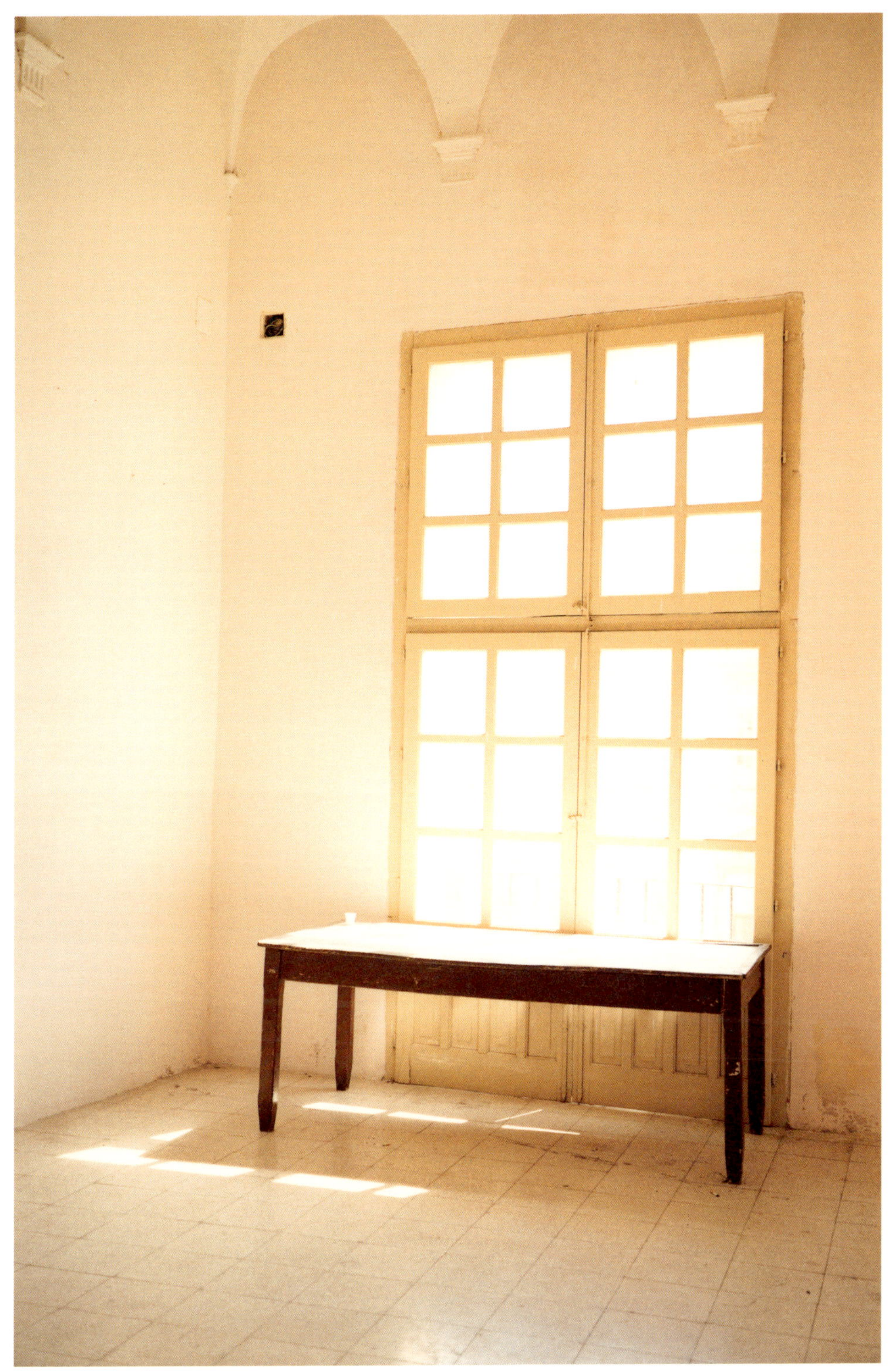

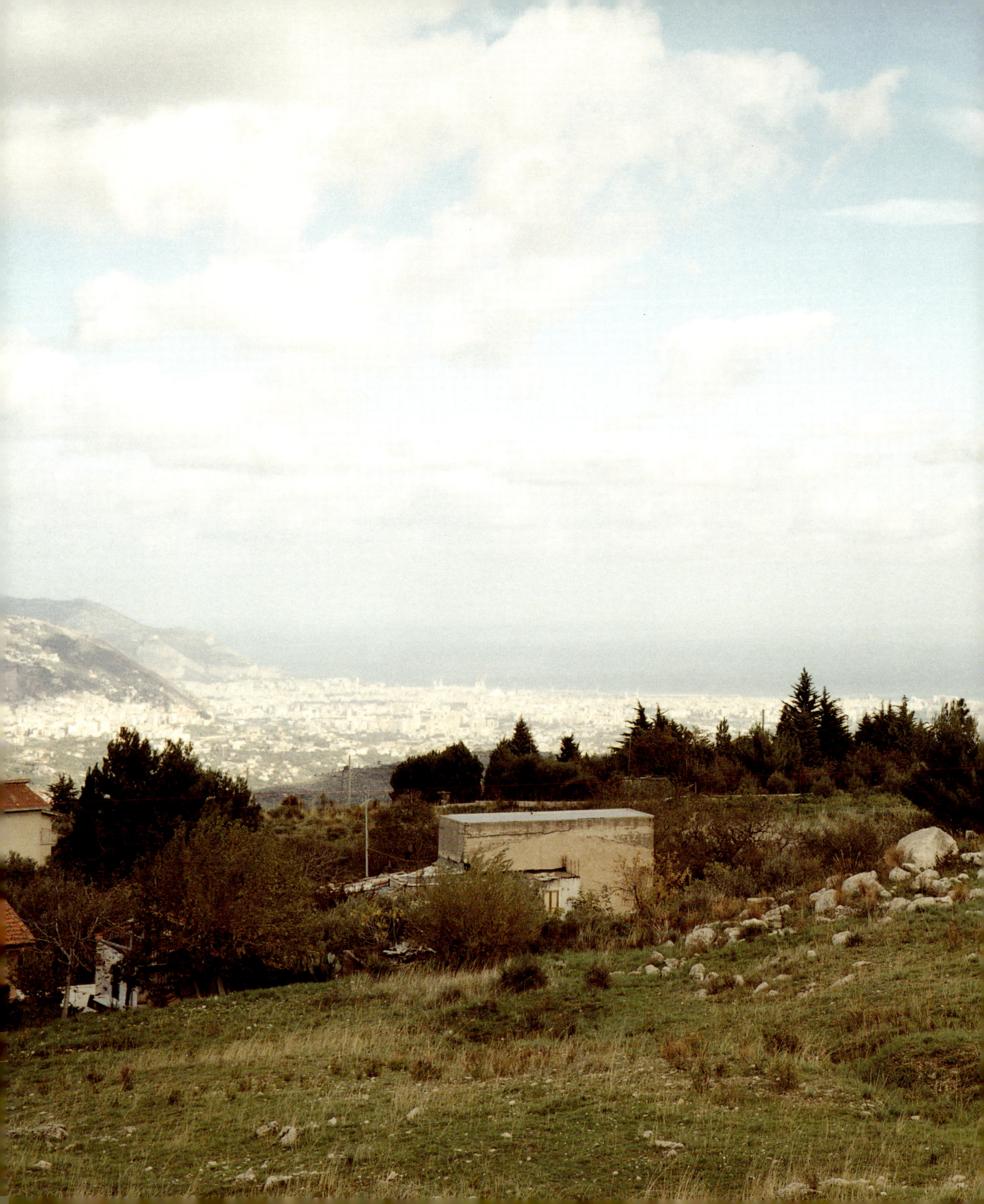

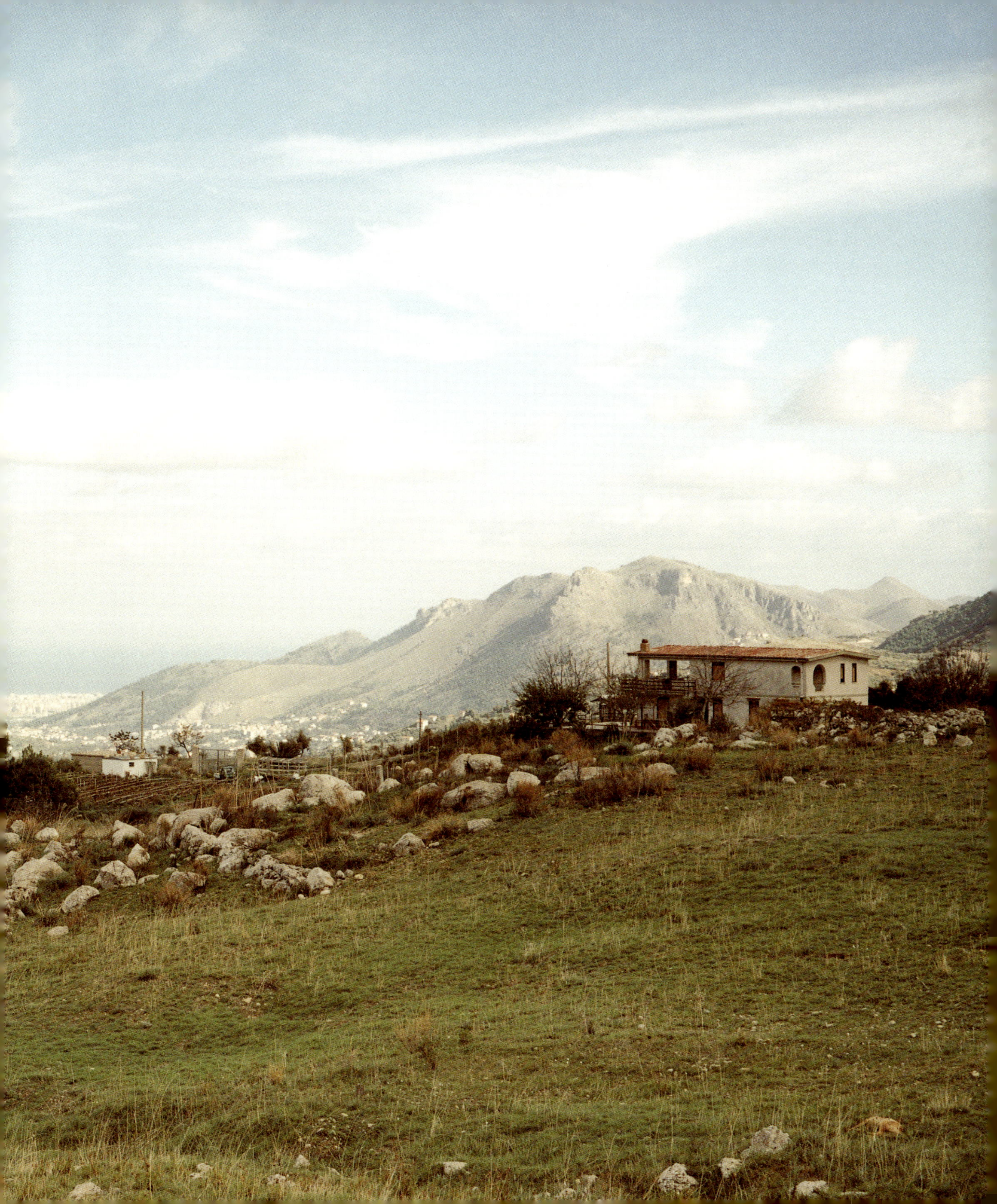

**Caltanissetta 28 April**

At last we can say we have seen with our own eyes the reason why Sicily earned the title of 'the granary of Italy'. Soon after Girgenti, the fertility began. There are no great level areas, but the gently rolling uplands were completely covered with wheat and barley in one great unbroken mass. Wherever the soil is suitable to their growth, it is so well tended and exploited that not a tree is to be seen. Even the small hamlets and other dwellings are confined to the ridges, where the limestone rocks make the ground untillable. The women live in these hamlets all year round spinning and weaving, but during the season of field labour, the men spend only Saturday and Sundays with them; the rest of the week they spend in the valleys and sleep at nights in reed huts. Our desire had certainly been granted; indeed, we soon came to long for the winged chariot of triptolemus to bear us away out of this monotony.

From Goethe *Italian Journey* (1786-1789)

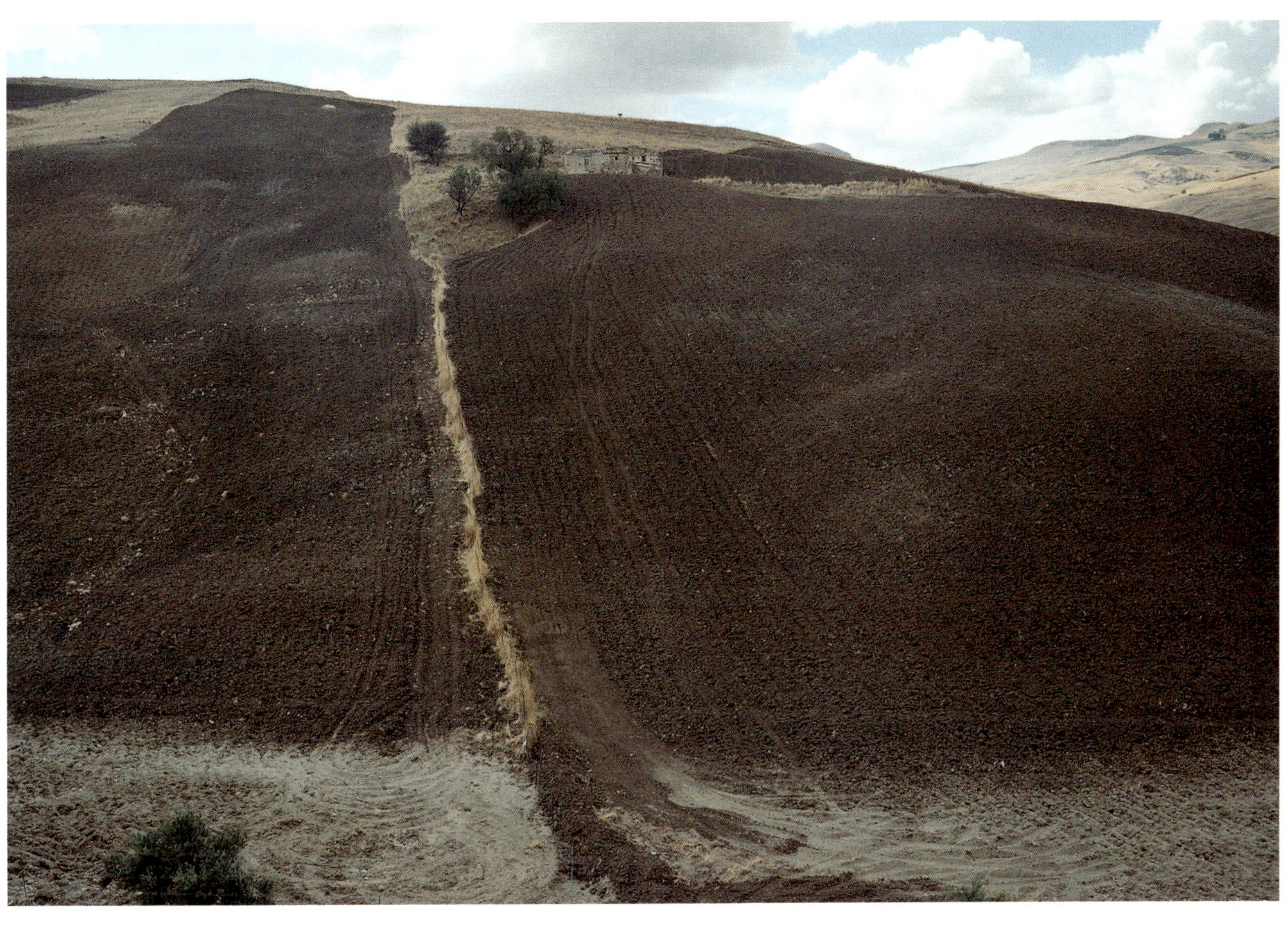

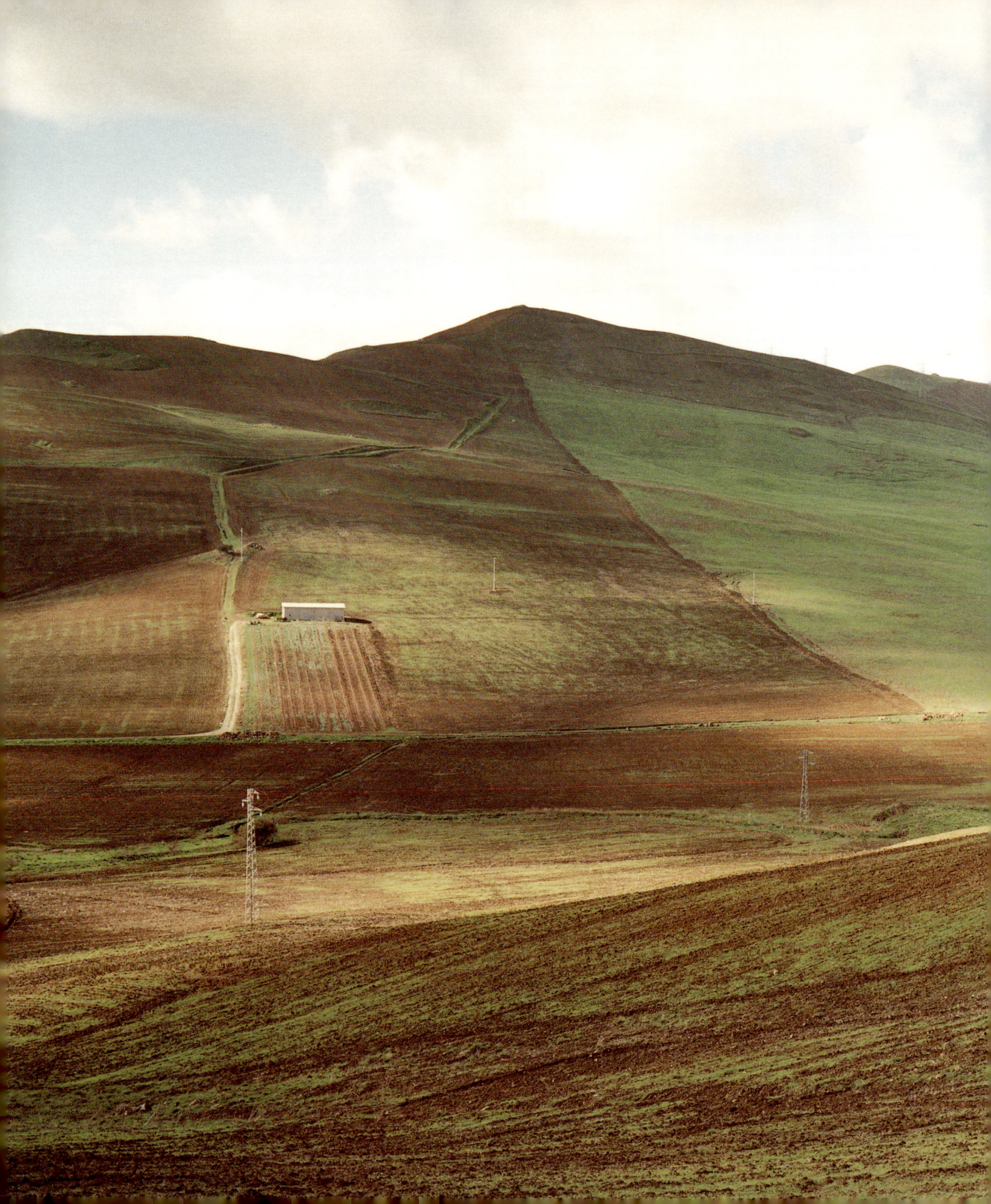

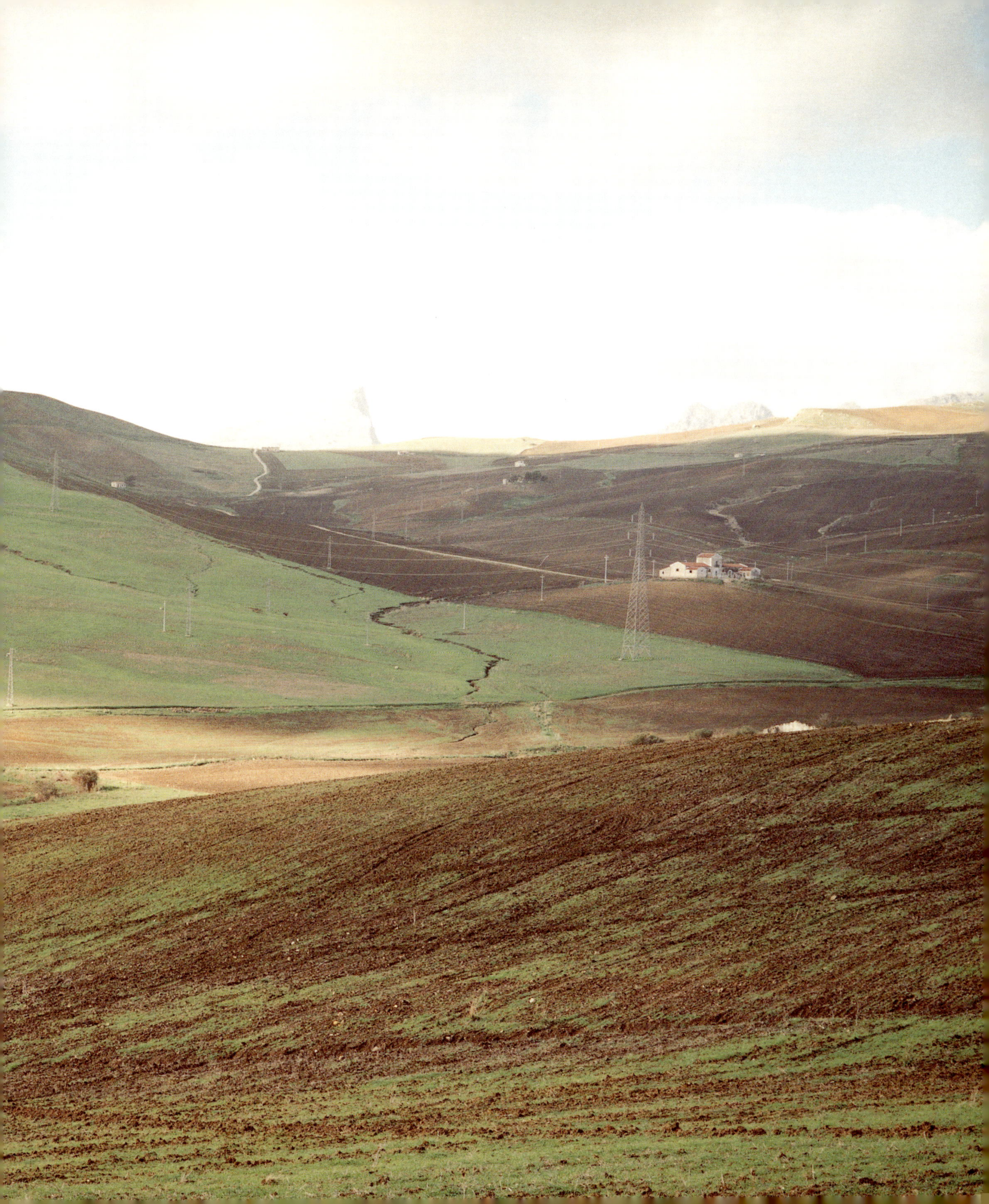

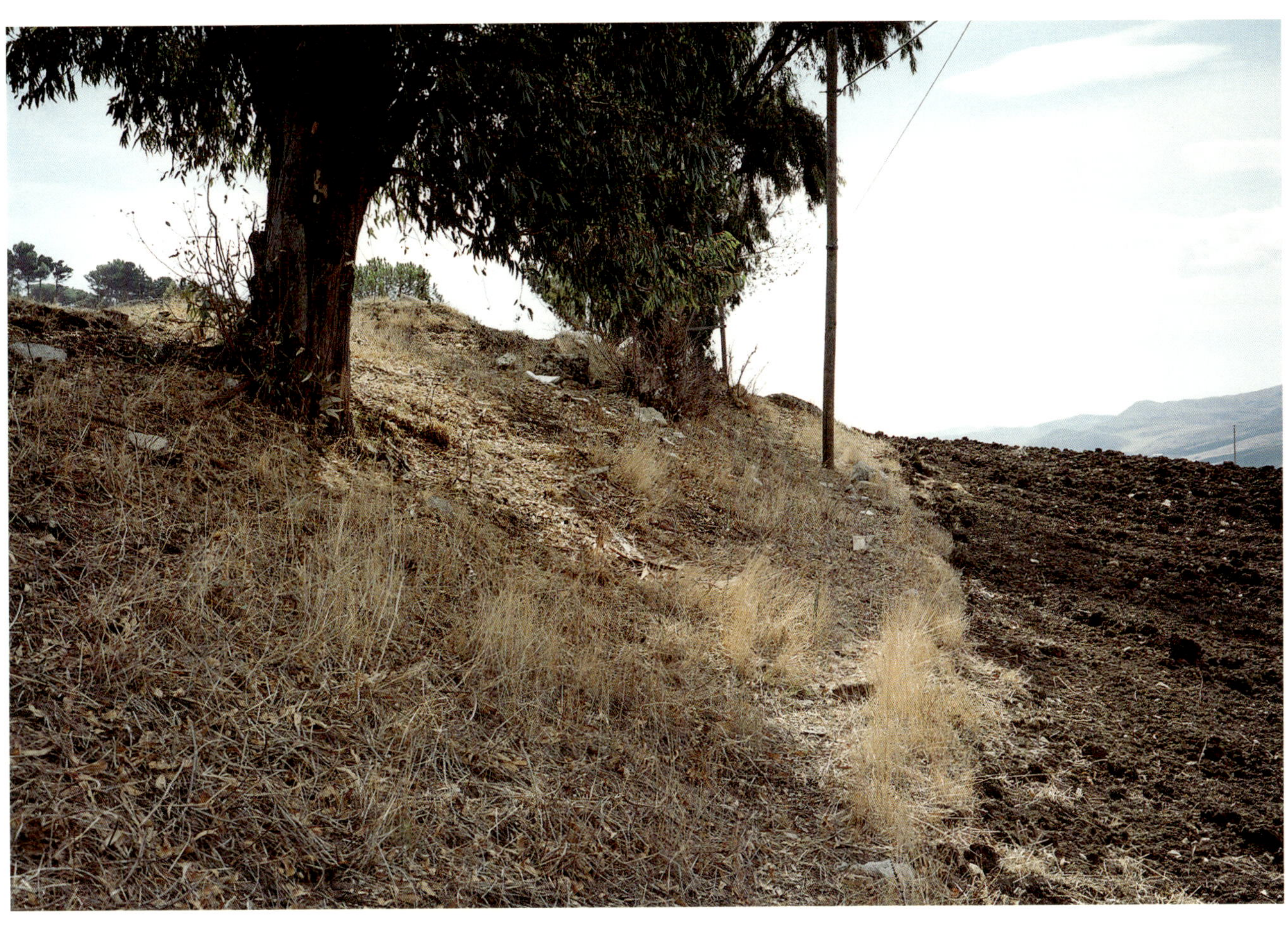

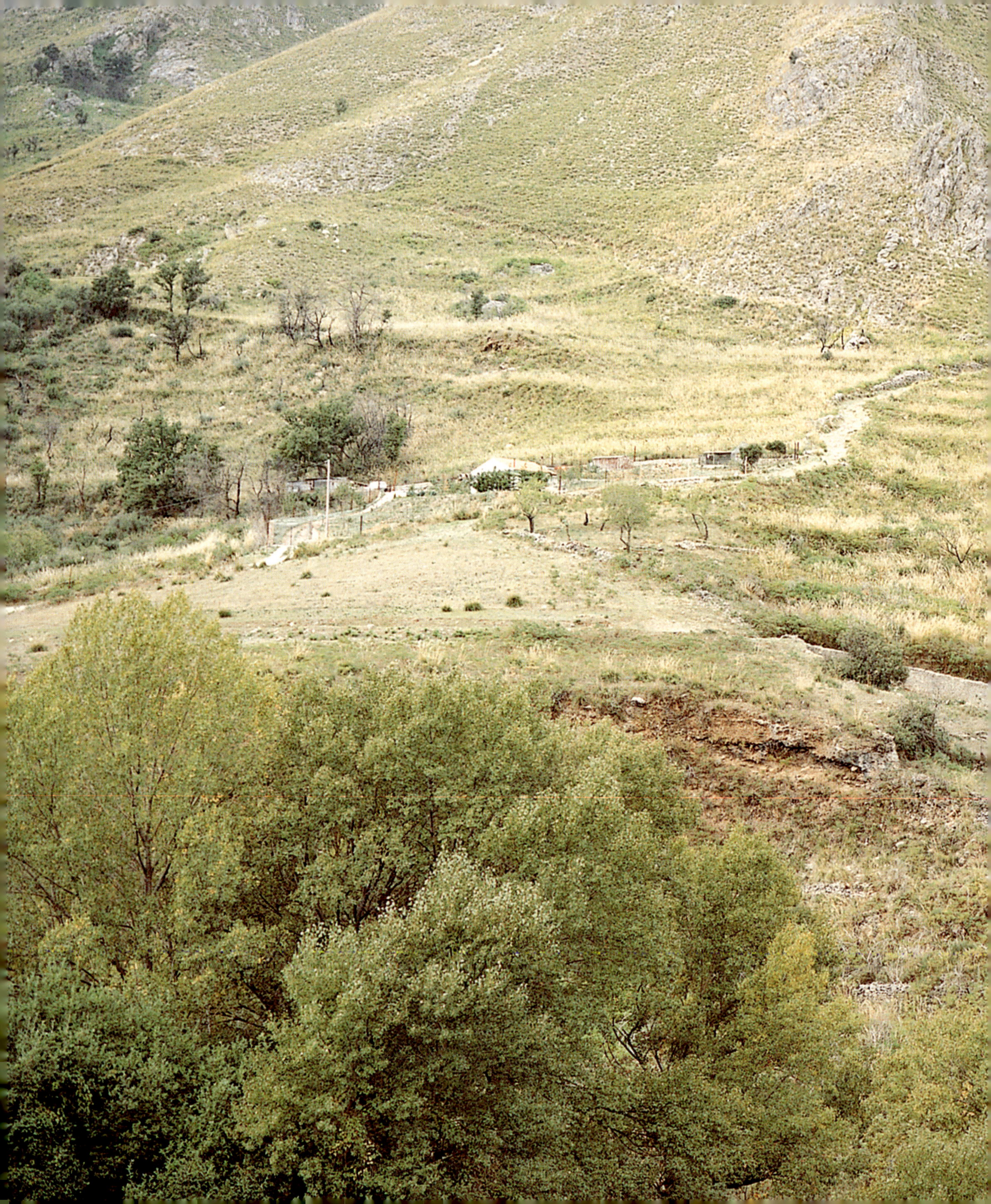

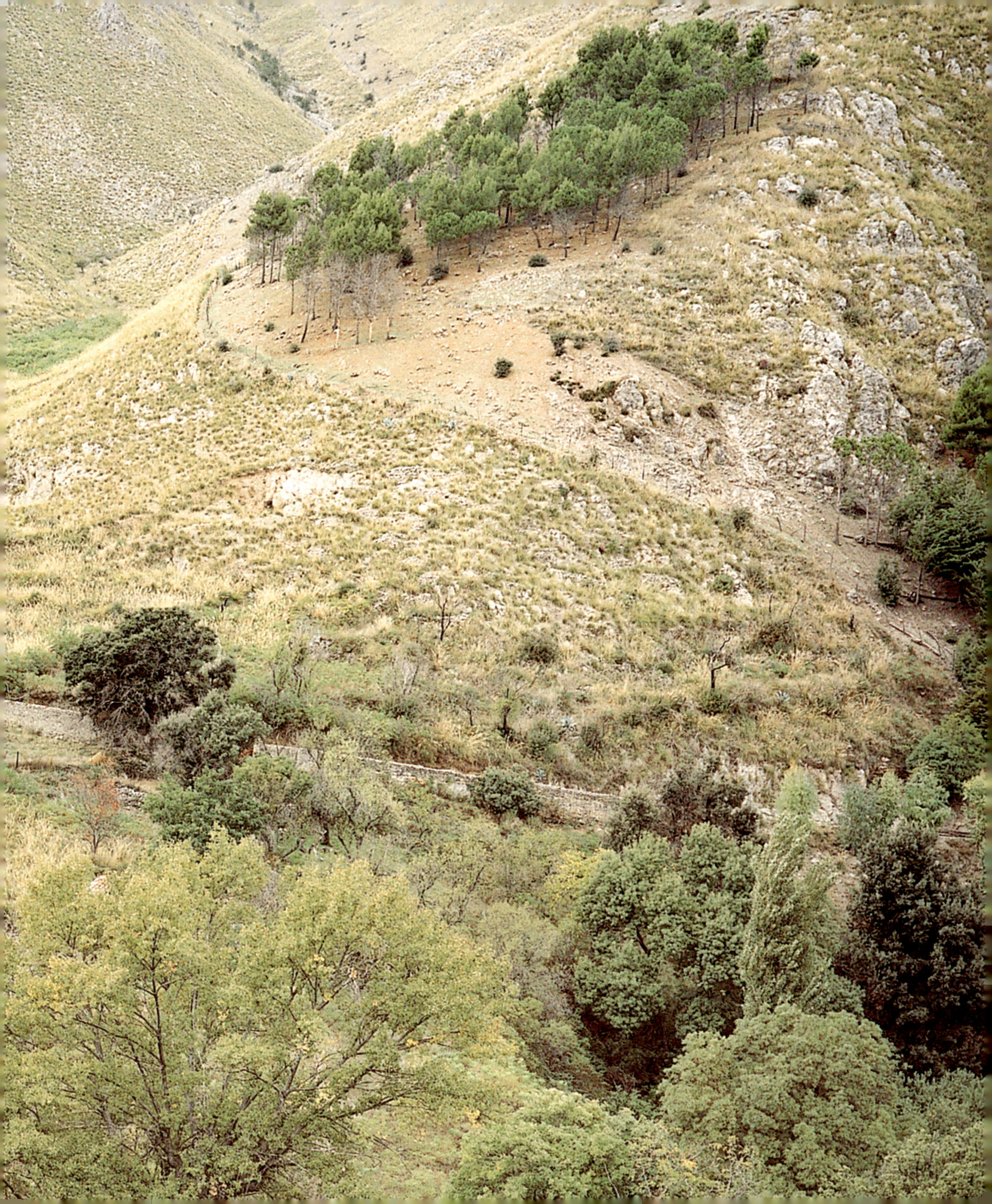

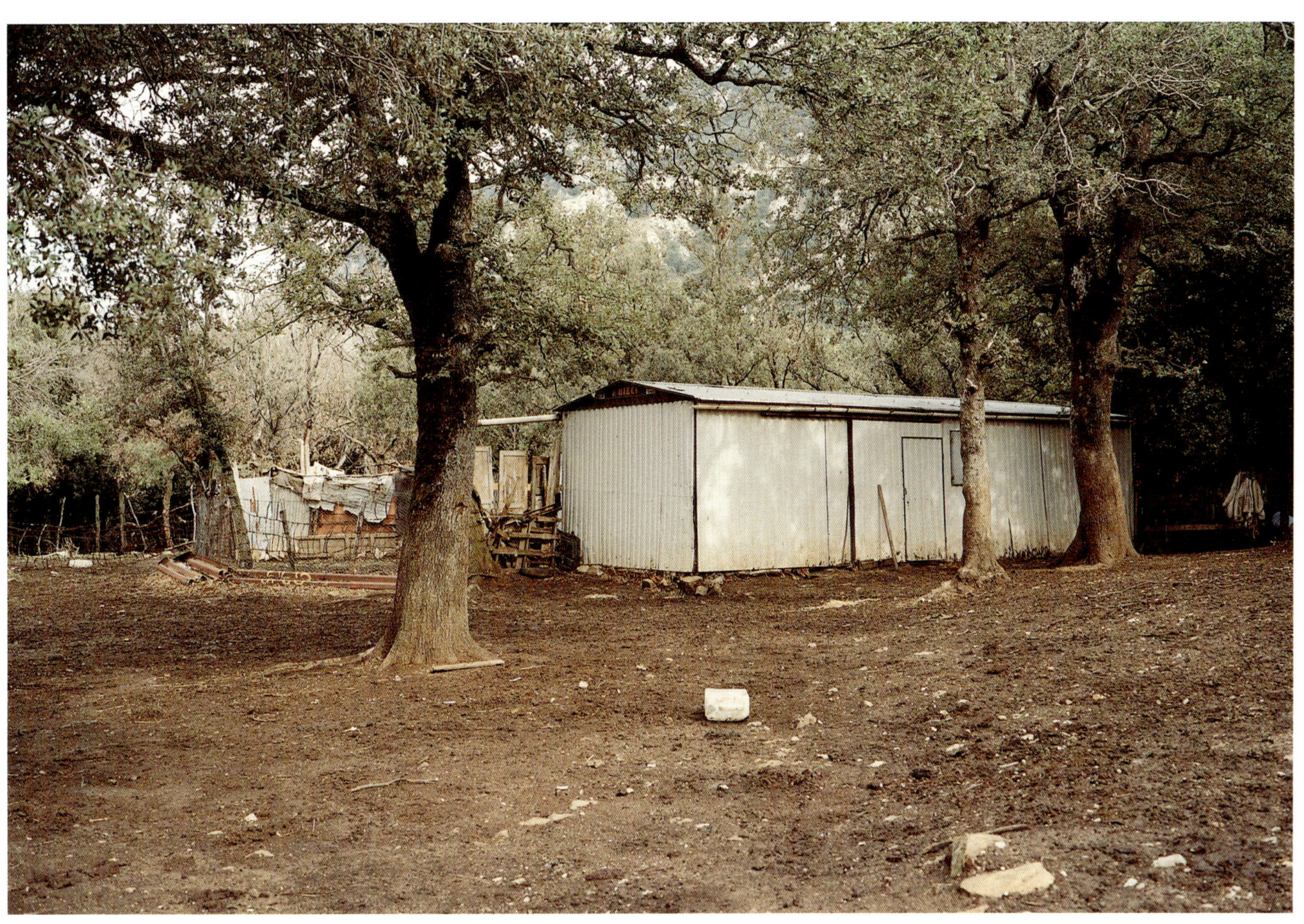

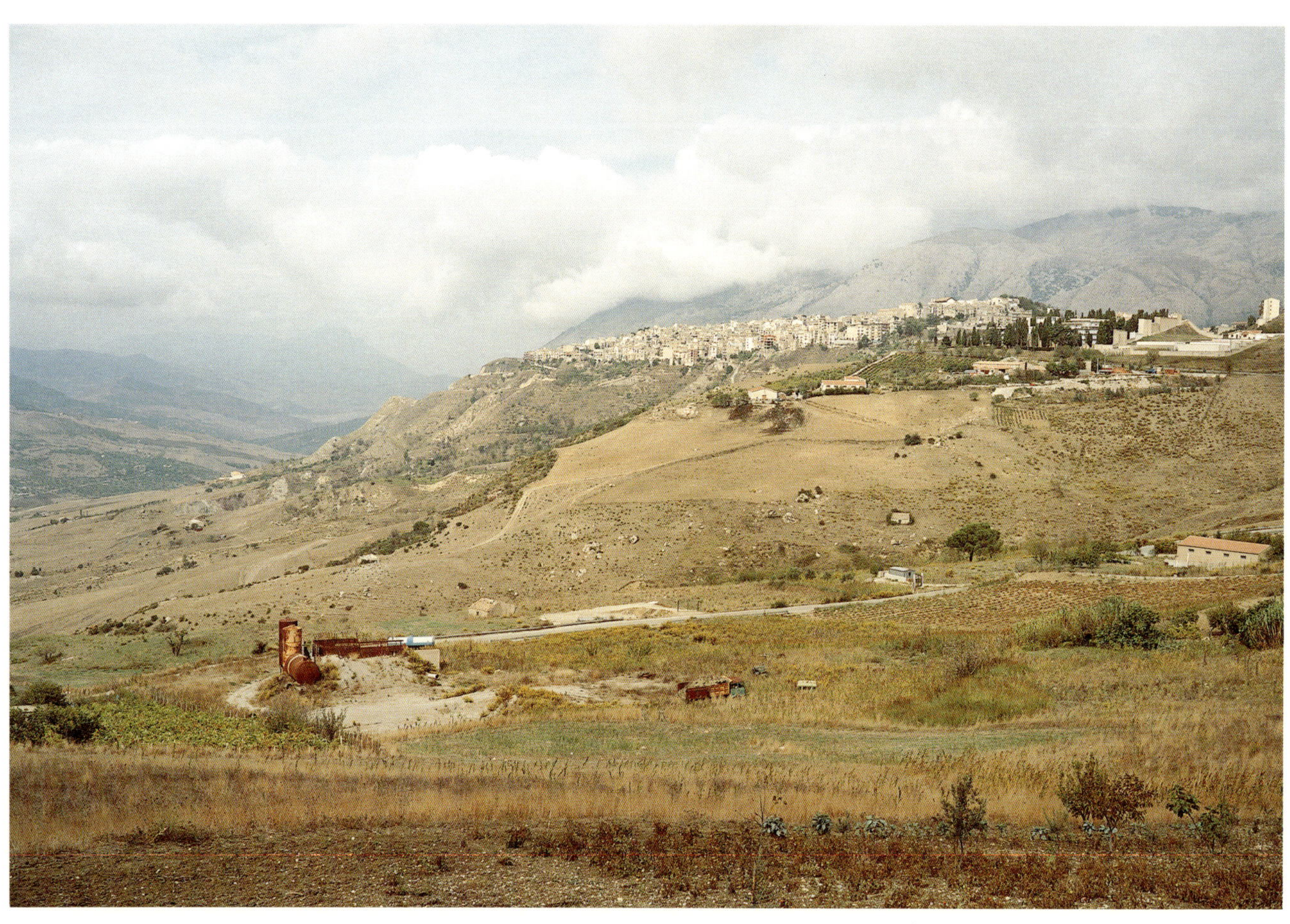

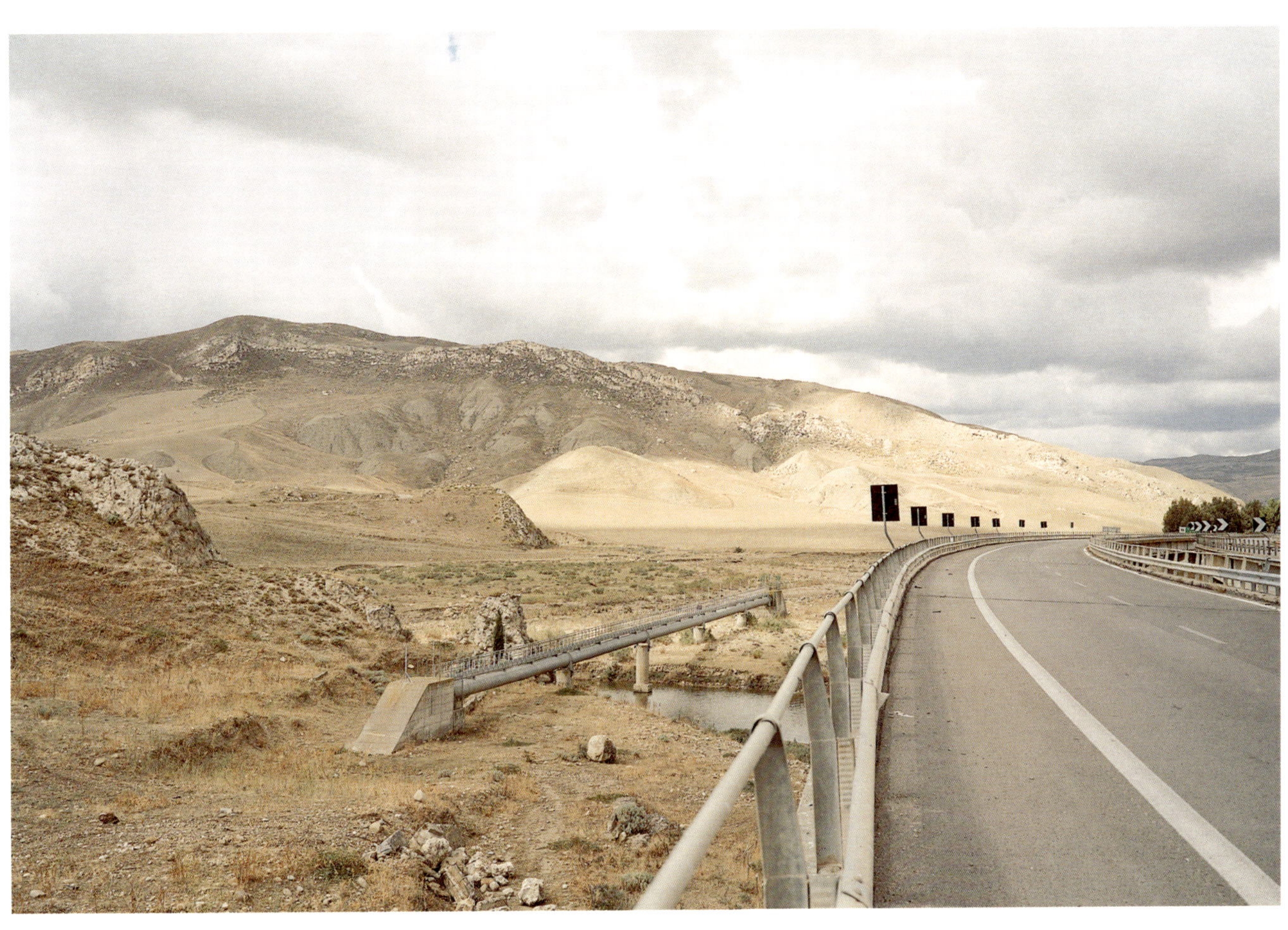

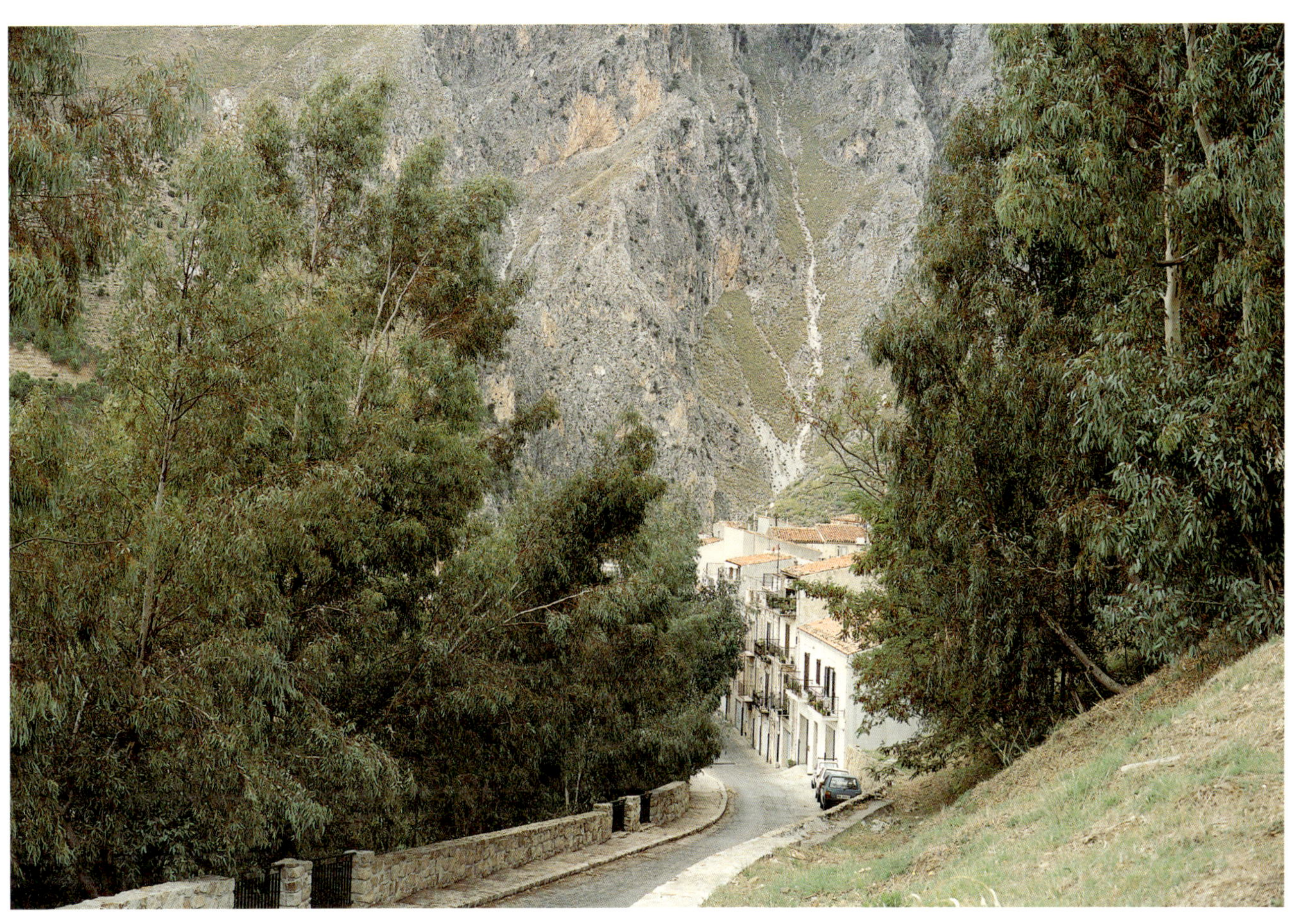

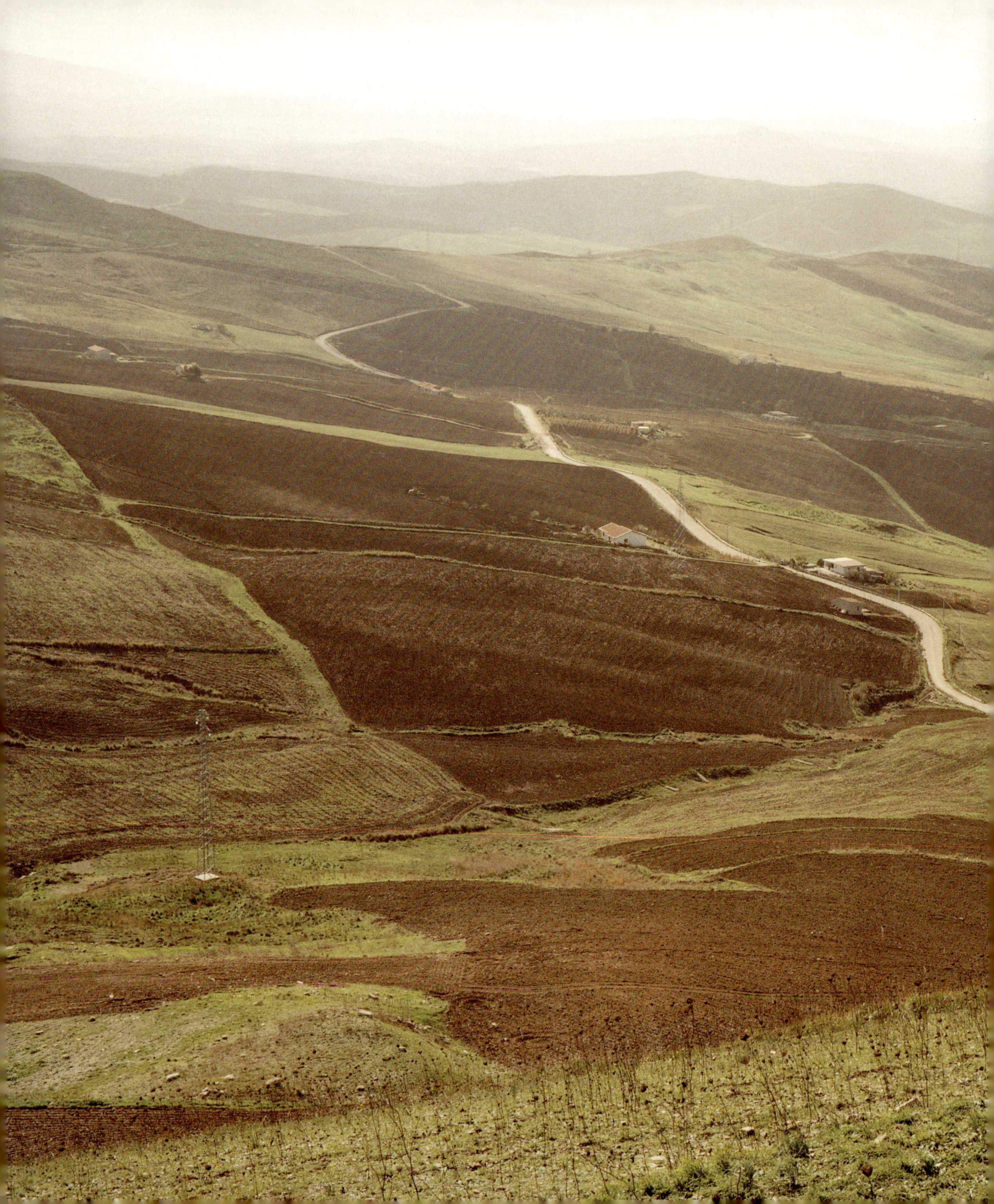

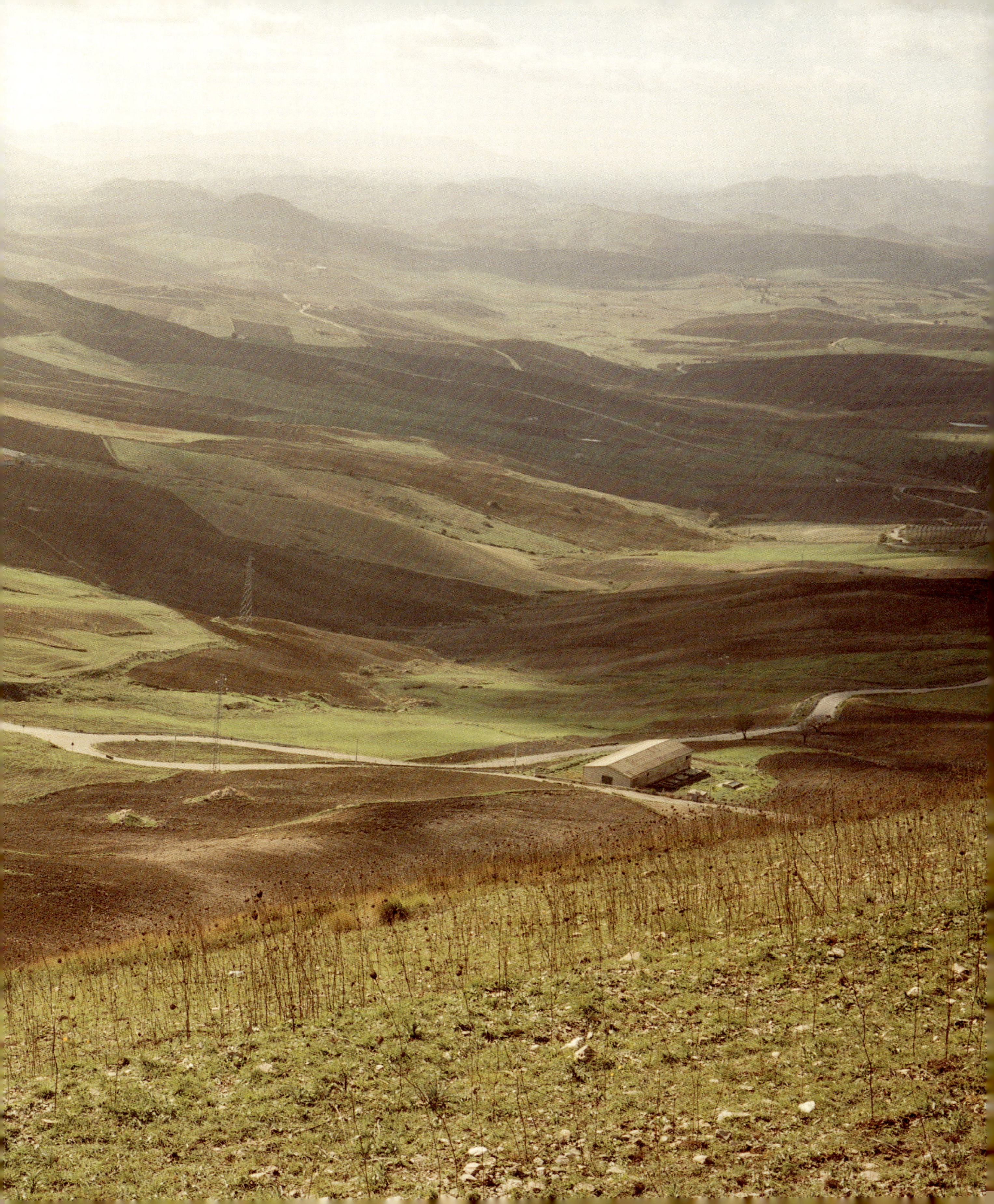

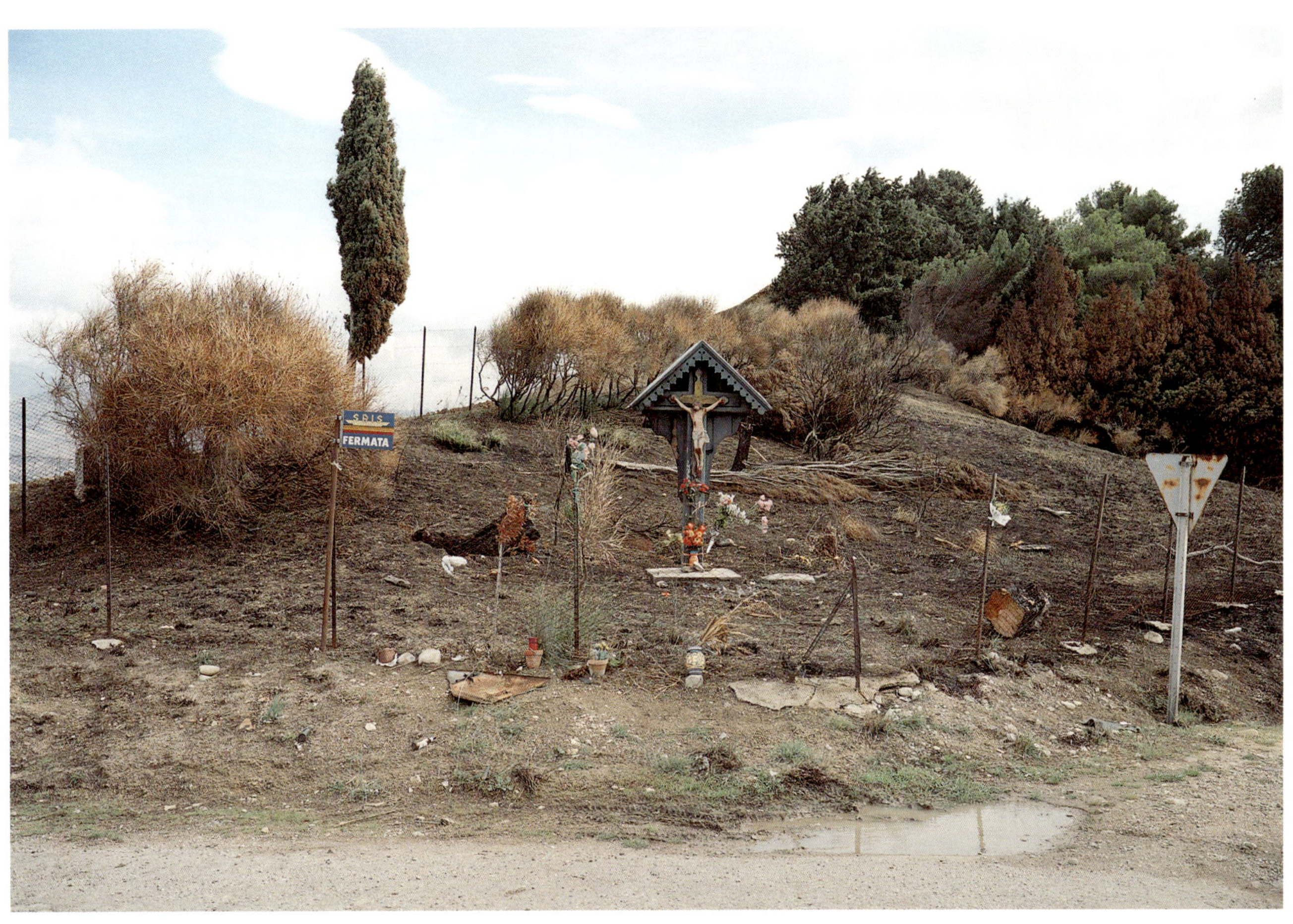
FERMATA

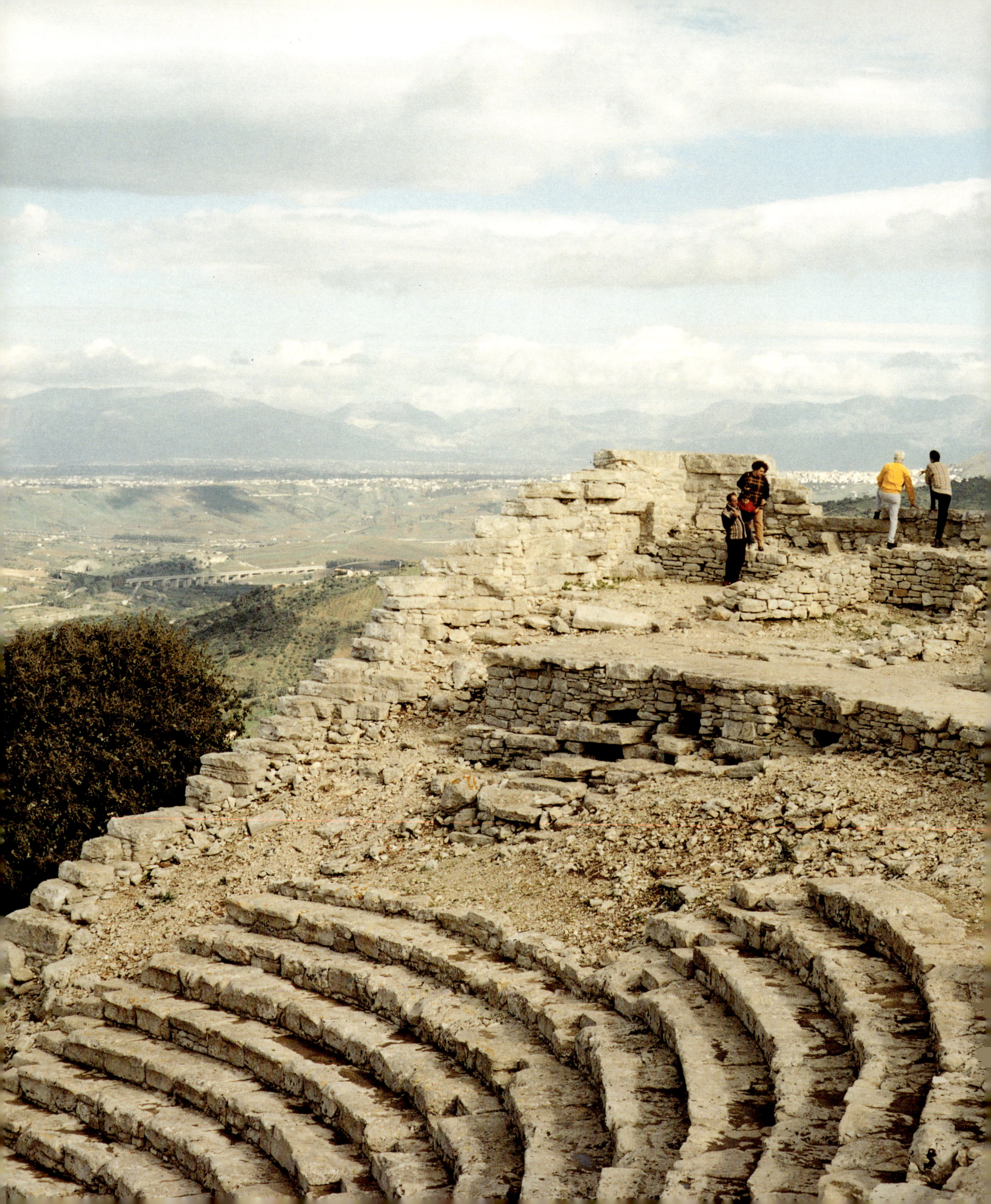

**I Siciliani**

Adrian Cole

On a steep road high in the Madonie Mountains – *Alte Madonie* – of northern Sicily, my brother is driving his rented Opel Vectra at ten miles an hour, peering through the windscreen at the terrain spread out before him. Fifteen hundred meters below are the fertile plains that made Sicily (in Cicero's estimation) the 'Granary of Rome'. These gargantuan fields roll away to the horizon, scarred by the deep etchings of erosion, heavy winter rains, flash floods. Their post-harvest browns mutate with the transformations of light into ochres and subtle sepia tones, and cloud shadows race across them. The steep sides of hills left un-ploughed, unploughable, offer up sharp and craggy outcroppings of rock interrupting the strenuous agriculture around them. Here and there the minute marks of human occupation: a shepherd's hut, a farm track, a switchback footpath carved by generations up to a hilltop shrine topped with a cross. On these plains humans have toiled for millennia, producing food for foreign masters.

Every few minutes my brother stops the car and cuts the engine. He gets out and walks to the side of the mountain, looking around, and manipulates his heavy Fuji six by nine. For the trip he brought thirty rolls of film which, owing to the size of the negative, only allow eight pictures per film. How possible would it be to capture the immensity of what's before him with anything less? He shoots a few frames and reloads the camera. Perhaps quarter of a mile ahead of him I am walking. This is a zigzag mountain road, so for a few hundred yards we are within sight of each other and in the still, Alpine air of the mountains I hear the diesel rattle of the car as it starts every few minutes and chugs uphill. Here there are few trees and little to break up the line of eye, just rocks and short coarse grass, the occasional starling, sparrow or lark and high up in the sky a hawk or two. From a neighbouring hillside comes the clank of bells around the necks of a herd of sheep. The mountains sweep up to a fine disappearing point on one side and on the other they build to a wave-like wall, which in its height and steepness seems about to topple over on me.

My reverie is broken by the noise of another car. A small white vehicle passes me, inside of which are three men, all unshaven and all with dark hair and hard leathery faces. The car is full of rust holes and completely devoid of exhaust. It slows down slightly and the men turn to stare at me, their heads still revolving owl-like as they pass and begin to pull away. We had left the last town, Polizzi Generosa, several miles and several thousand feet behind us. Polizzi Generosa earned its name from its relationship to earlier religious figures – Polis Isis to the ancients. The Bourbon Emperor Frederick gave it the suffix Generosa for being generous – with blood and money – at the time of the Arab revolts. Sitting on its rocky spur beneath the Western range of the Madonie, it shared with many interior Sicilian towns one overriding characteristic: impregnability.

If Sicily is, true to stereotype, and as many Sicilians admit (after decades of denial) full of Mafiosi killers, kidnappers and thugs, then I wondered what would prevent these men from stopping their car, killing us both and helping themselves to our things? They didn't immediately bring to mind tourist-inspired images of tables laden with fresh produce surrounded by smiling families breaking bread to the goddess of *la Bella Italia*. But then many benign images of Italy do not apply in Sicily. The car continued on its way, wherever it was going, and the occupants clearly decided to live with the enigma of a couple

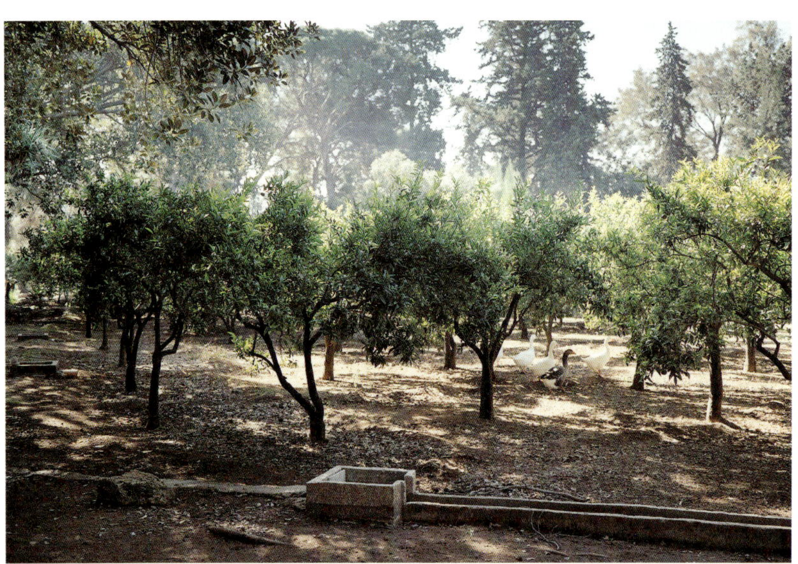

of crazy foreigners, or perhaps decided to run from the two dark strangers who were setting up some violent act.

II.

I remembered the way those men in the small white car looked at me as they passed: their eyes were full of a dull kind of suspicion, their look inscrutable yet deathly curious. Could they have accepted that I was enjoying stretching my legs, that I was greatly enjoying the views, the air, the sounds of the mountains? On this island people want to know what you are doing, and yet simultaneously and for very concrete reasons they don't. This is after all, and as my brother informs me frequently, Sicily. He doesn't say this to remind himself of his whereabouts; what he means is that things are different here, life operates according to different rules, rules that are strictly and uniquely Sicilian. I am here to assist him on a photographic mission to capture some interior Sicilian landscapes and as he's much more familiar with the island than I am his assertions have to hold weight. I myself know nothing of the island, but for years now I have heard his tales about it: the decadent vivacity of Palermo; the compromised yet effervescent population; the centuries of glory – Greek, Roman, Arab, Norman – all but forgotten today; the insistent and broiling heat relieved only by the deep rocky coves of the Mediterranean; islands with lyrical and quixotic names: Lampedusa, Pantelleria, Stromboli, Favignana. And, then, of course, there is the Mafia.

I always felt, frankly, that my brother's Mafia talk was somewhat exaggerated fantasy, a story-telling prop. He'd regale me with descriptions of 'obvious killers' sitting in the departure lounge of Palermo airport surrounded by lackeys paying homage. These were always huge men whose descriptions brought to mind Bela Lugosi. They had hands the size of dinner plates, scars across their necks from assassination attempts. And then the eyes, always the eyes. Like dead fish.

Like sharks. In summer there were more of them, perhaps because it was one of the only air-conditioned places in town, yet still the terrible heat, the rage-inducing heat forced rivers of sweat to run down their murderous faces. And he knew they were the killers, there was no question. He knew because he was familiar with Sicily. Other tourists might have walked past them, ignorant in the presence of evil, blithely unaware and charmed to be in Italy. But he had achieved a level of knowledge about this place that rendered such naiveté impossible. I was skeptical. Not of the Mafia's activities and presence, but perhaps of their visibility. Although, according to reports from police informants in the last decade, there probably numbered over five thousand 'men of honour' in Sicily, I doubted they'd be standing around on street corners.

In our journey across Sicily I had the opportunity to see for myself what Martin had been talking about all these years. I witnessed the way in which my brother had begun to see under the filmy surface of a society, and to read between the lines. In my brother's opinion it was Sicily's rampant social malaise which made the place so interesting, gave it flavor, dimension, ambiguity. If landscapes have a meaning, it must be connected to the people who inhabit them, no matter how sparsely, and to how that landscape has been used throughout history – to what happened there. I wanted to see in what way was it accurate to see Sicily as permeated by the culture of crime, as most outsiders are led to believe, and asked myself, was the relationship between crime and Sicily like the stereotypical one between Ireland and alcohol? In the latter case some people argue that social drinking in an alcohol culture should not be considered alcoholism, even if people routinely sink five pints a night at the pub. Was Sicily's criminal organisation a logical extension of its specific cultural attributes? If so, one would be able to detect the 'small m' mafia in everything. We talk about 'mafias' to refer to groups that are exclusive and compulsively, anti-socially promoting their own interests. Is the criminal Mafia simply an extension of this tendency to keep it in the tribe, to the exclusion of the wider society and, in Sicily's case, the state?

Landscape was central to Martin's understanding of the Mafia, and to Sicily in general: 'I could go to Scotland and take beautiful 'vistas' of the Isle of Skye, or of Loch Lomand, they'd just be pretty pictures of... Scotland. The point is that you know that just beyond that cairn, or behind that lake, some Sloan is walking his Labrador in his oiled Barber and green wellies'. In Europe it is often hard to meet isolation, both physical and social. You know that somewhere close by is a shopping mall, a friendly pub or a youth hostel. Sicily, according to my brother's view, offers some raw isolation and some pockets of history into which you can wander and feel the qualitative change. It is Europe, but it can seem as vast and desolate and raw as Turkmenistan.

The author Norman Lewis also sees a connection between these areas. Talking about Villalba, an infamous Mafia stronghold in Sicily's interior, he says: 'Central Asia must be like this, one imagines. There are no boundaries, hedges, walls, trees, windmills, buildings of any kind. The landscape, green for weeks of spring and thereafter whiteish under the sun, heaves gently like a carpet with the wind under it'. I recently saw a spread of photos of Scotland in my local Starbucks in Massachusetts. The photographer was grasping for wildness and beauty, but in order to evoke it referred more to the Hollywood movie Braveheart than modern Scotland, which is a pleasant, easy, connected tourist destination. (All over the Paris Metro you can see grainy black and white photos of a young couple in a vintage car driving along the side of a loch). And how wild and beautiful can a place be which is pleasant, easy and connected? Beauty and wildness must contain an element of awe. In Scotland they do not have a method of killing known as *La Capra* (The Goat), in which the victim has his legs and arms tied together behind his back, with a rope attached to his neck; in struggling to get free, he chokes himself to death. And what imagery is this if not imagery from the world of the peasant – the goatherd? Imagery directly connected to the island's long and very feudal past that still lives on in the mountain top shrines, the tiny straw shepherd's huts, the corroded landscape. And this imagery of death and animal husbandry relates not just to an earlier period of human evolution, or from the time of Braveheart, but from well into the nineteen eighties and probably up until today.

III.

Martin had been introduced to Sicily by his wife, Aithne. She had spent a couple of years there teaching English after university. Her time on the island had been hard, as it often is for a foreigner abroad, and slightly traumatic. This was partly due to the timing. In the eighties Palermo was in the grip of a Mafia war, the effects of which were broadly experienced in Sicilian society. And when the 'maxi trials' of Mafia bosses began, Palermo had the feeling of a city under siege. The army had been mobilised in Sicily and Palermo street corners bristled with soldiers and tanks. Assassinations were a daily occurrence. For a major city in one of Europe's biggest nations it was an extreme and bizarre situation. Aithne's Sicilian friends and colleagues all suffered from some sort of fallout from this period; a sense of stress and fatigue gripped the city. Men in the streets made obscene, provocative gestures at women, like helpless small boys in desperate need of attention. Middle class, well dressed men, masturbating on a park bench.

Nonetheless, when Aithne spoke to Martin of Sicily some years later, she was still full of wonder and excitement about the island. Martin, who had done his fair share of travelling, including stints in Asia and Africa, was not convinced that a Mediterranean island belonging to Italy could really provide much in the way of exotica, otherness, thrill, or whatever he was then looking for from travel. On their first visit, though, Martin was quick to see why she had become so taken with it and soon became totally enraptured himself. He has been coming here long enough now to feel genuinely galled when a Sicilian marks him out as a foreigner. This often, in his own take on it, entails some sort of disrespect. I was interested to hear my brother use this quintessentially Mediterranean term. Over the course of a week or so travelling on the island

I witnessed a strange transformation from my normally slightly phlegmatic northern European sibling, as he began adopting some of the values of our hosts, becoming paradoxically vulnerable and stronger. Vulnerable because, with knowledge (as Eliot said), 'what forgiveness?' And stronger, through that self-same knowledge.

In his previous trips to the island he had often been mistaken for a native because of his dark hair and the fact that there are not many tourists in Sicily. On the plane from Rome to Palermo he told me about a bus ride he and Aithne had taken once near Trapani. He had become ensnared in a staring match with a young man who looked exactly like Mel Gibson: short and stocky with extremely intense green-blue eyes. At first it was just a friendly smile or two, but he found it difficult for some reason to disengage from the man's stare, and realised that he had entered into anthropological territory that he could not navigate. Was it sexual? Hostile? Hospitable? To his discomfort the man got up from his seat and came to sit in the vacant aisle seat next to him. His forearms were emblazoned with tattoos depicting lightening bolts. They were etched on to the arm in the same way in which kill symbols are painted on the fuselages of fighter planes during wartime. The significance of this was not lost on Martin: the man had done something numerous times. The man started babbling away, apparently mistaking Martin for somebody from Trapani. 'But you are Trapanesi, aren't you?', he kept on saying. His tone was defensive and he seemed to feel that Martin was following him because he repeatedly saw him. When Aithne joined the conversation to tell the man that Martin was, in fact, an English tourist from London, he scoffed at the suggestion, saying: 'he's no more from London than I am from Catania!' Several tense minutes elapsed in which the man, teetering between anger and confusion, tried to figure out if he was being made fun of, then he got up and returned to his seat.

Often in Sicily a stranger can blunder his way into a labyrinth of seemingly ancient and inexplicable grievances, unpredictable and dangerous situations. And it is in this context that travel poses an existential dilemma. For so much of human history, meaning has been generated from our geography. The fact is that we are genetically programmed for geography, designed for location, place-specific. It was inconceivable to this man that my brother was a tourist because you very rarely saw tourists on local buses in this part of Sicily. What would an outsider be doing there?

Being mistaken for a local, however, is always a great compliment, and this was not the only time it happened to Martin. Other encounters revealed different aspects of Sicilian culture, often more benign ones. And whereas the Trapani experience was jarring, these were endearing, if a little weird. The case of the elderly swimmer, for example, had Martin musing on gender relations in Sicily. Swimming in a rocky cove near Palermo one day, he felt his leg being tickled by something underwater, then, as he looked down to see what it was, he felt a hand grab his knee. He thrashed the water and kicked his legs, and next to him the head of an elderly man broke the surface, and his wrinkled face burst into laughter. The old man, bobbing up and down started to chatter away in the Sicilian dialect. My brother smiled at him and told him he was a foreigner, at which the old man looked horrified and made for the shore. 'The question is', said Martin, 'would it have been normal for him to have done this to a Sicilian stranger, would a Sicilian have understood and participated in his frolicking?'.

IV.

Falcone Borsellino airport lies along the coast from Palermo, nestled under a thousand-metre cliff which rises in a wing-like sweep over the sea. We arrived from Rome, after a turbulent flight, filling the passengers with tension as they nervously looked at the thunderheads and cumulii nimbus spread out above the Italian skies, the Appennine backbone of Italy acting as a lightening rod for cloud-cover. On the way out of the airport I noticed a poster stuck to a wall near the men's lavatory. It had a crudely photo-copied picture of a young man of about nineteen. Underneath were the words 'Please Help Me Find My Son', in big letters. Then a paragraph of text which turned out to be a heart-felt plea from an English father, for any information about his son's disappearance: 'My son loved your country. That is why he visited it frequently, and spent his time visiting churches and your historic landmarks. I just want to know if he was involved in an accident, or whatever happened, as is a father's right to know'. Martin came and looked at it.

'I bet he saw something he shouldn't have.' Martin said.

He told me how several years ago he and Aithne had been picnicking in a wooded glade in the hills not far from Palermo. Nearby was some kind of building that they assumed was perhaps an olive oil bottling plant. As they sat on the ground eating, a large black Mercedes pulled up outside the building, having followed the rough farm track there. Out stepped four extremely well dressed men, and while two of them went inside the building, two stood and stared at them intently for several minutes. Both Martin and Aithne felt they were in the wrong place, but tried their hardest to look the innocent honeymooning couple; soon the two men wrenched their stare away from them and went inside.

'This boy was probably wondering around in the country and saw someone get killed, or a body being dumped.' Martin mused, looking at the poster. 'He didn't have an accident. If you have an accident someone sees it or someone finds the body, not this silence and mystery.'

We made for the Avis car rental office. There were several groups of people renting cars, most of them Americans. Behind the counter a middle-aged, wiry man with precise English was holding at bay a large line, while a younger woman named Paula was developing a bad attitude with a German couple. As this relationship disintegrated under the twin pressures of linguistic incompatibility and unequal expectations, Martin told me about Atillo who usually manned this office and of his fear of seeing him today. Two years previously he and Aithne had rented a car from him and lost the keys while swimming. On being given another car, a brand new Lancia, Martin, in a fit of heat and claustrophobia-induced rage, propelled it through an impossibly narrow gap in the old city removing the wing mirrors and door handles. Even then, he was becoming a Palermitano.

Punta Raisi was the former name of the airport until, in the 1990s, its was renamed after two anti-mafia prosecutors both of whom were murdered in Sicily in that decade. Giovanni Falcone was assassinated on the road from the airport to Palermo, when he was returning unannounced from Rome for the weekend. A bomb blew a twenty-foot deep crater in the road, catapulting the lead car across the highway into an orchard, and ripping apart the front section of Falcone's £90,000 bullet-proof Fiat Croma. Paolo Borsellino, a childhood friend of Falcone and his closest colleague in the anti-Mafia tribunal in Palermo, stepped into Falcone's shoes as the lead anti-Mafia prosecutor. Borsellino lasted two

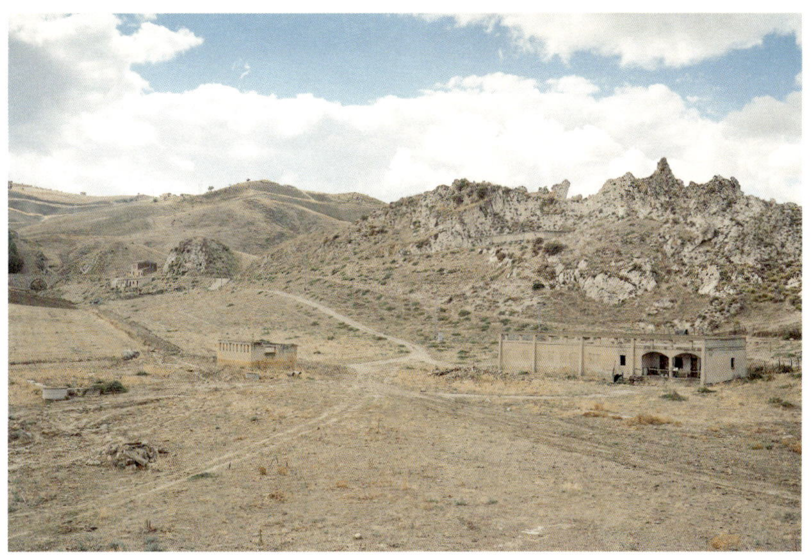

months in this position, and on July 19, 1992, on a trip to visit his mother, a car bomb killed him and his five police escorts. According to his daughter, Borsellino knew that if Falcone was killed, he would go too, as he used to say: 'Giovanni's my shield against *Cosa Nostra*. They'll kill him first, then they'll kill me.'

Falcone-Borsellino is a salutary entry-point into Sicily. The point is not lost on a visitor that first, Sicily is a place that has suffered greatly from its world famous home-grown organised crime, and second, that it is not lying down and taking it anymore. Falcone made important breakthroughs in understanding the structure of the Sicilian mob, strides made largely through the testimony of Pentiti, or supergrasses who decided to speak after the Mafia wars of the eighties when their lives looked (even for Mafiosi) particularly bleak and hopeless. It was this testimony that allowed Falcone to put together prosecution cases that in the maxi-trials of the eighties put hundreds of Mafia bosses and foot-soldiers, regular men of honor, behind bars. It also enabled the prosecutors to produce a detailed picture of the Mafia and see it as a hierarchical and organised body of criminals. Before this it had been assumed an amorphous group of families with similar value structures and a common distaste for the state. Soon after Falcone's murder, Savlatore (Toto) Riina, known as *la Belva*, (The Beast), and Italy's most wanted man, was arrested in Palermo where he'd been in hiding for twenty years. Falcone had said, a year before his murder: 'My account with *Cosa Nostra* remains open, I'll settle it with my death, natural or otherwise.' Even if he was gone and *Cosa Nostra* was short one more enemy his work was having its effect after his – unnatural – death.

From the airport we drove along the coast and away from Palermo on the same road (A29)

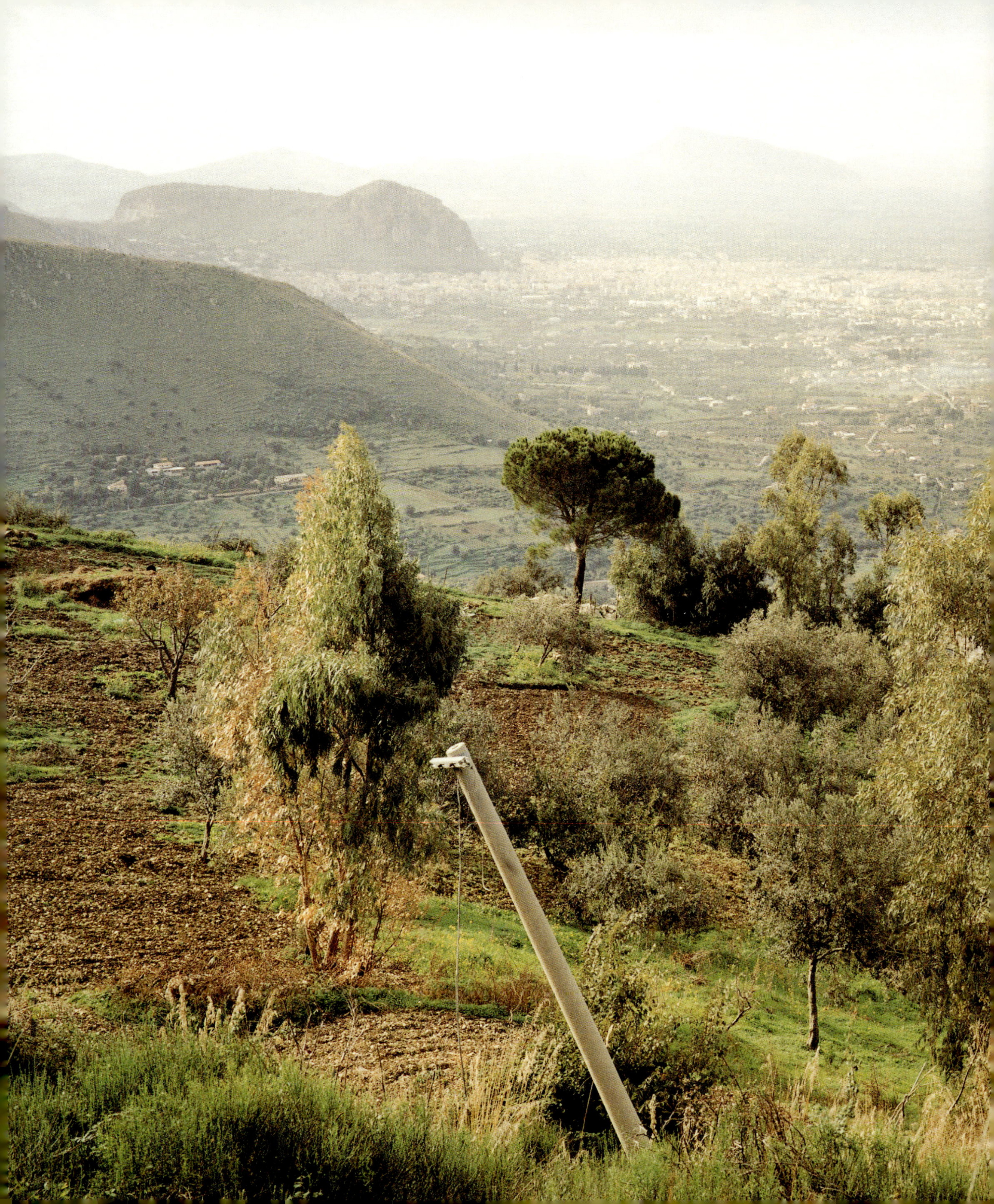

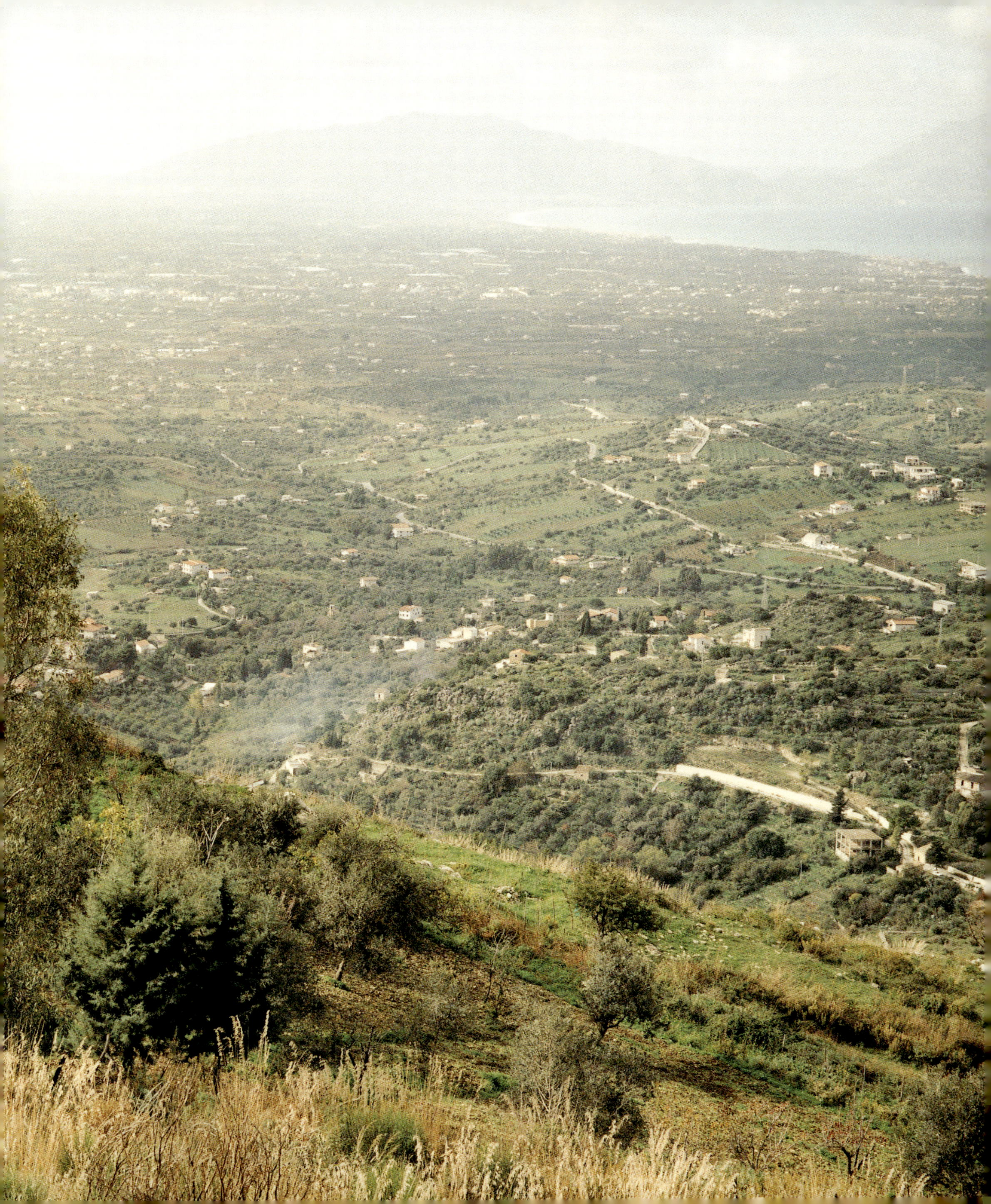

where Falcone had died, and headed for Alcamo where Martin said there was a natural hot springs with volcanically heated sulphurous waters that were good for relaxing in after a flight. It was getting dark and all I could make out of the landscape was the ominous shadows of mountains rising quite sharply from the sea. Above them dark clouds were gathering. On one road sign indicating Falcone-Borsellino airport someone had blacked out the names of the two murdered judges. We turned onto a dirt path which ran alongside a railway track. I could dimly make out in the fields collections of short wiry plants that were the vines, stretching across the valley floor until the land ascended steeply and turned into a sheer mountain side. Eventually we came to a compound where a few small Fiats were parked under some Eucalyptus trees. In the lobby of the house there was a TV playing the news and a couple of young men sitting around talking. The pool was like a regular swimming pool except that the temperature was that of a hot bath, and from it emanated the mild eggy smell of sulphur.

It was dark by now and quite cool, the mid-October wind coming from the north, not, this time, blowing hot sandy air from the Sahara away to the south of us. There was one man swimming around like a sleepy shark in the tepid water. Steam rose into the night air and in the distance I could make out the face of the mountain across the valley. The lone swimmer was chatty, as it turned out, and on learning that we were English started regaling us with tales of his one trip to England, twenty years ago. He was a junior post office official in Palermo then and went to Oxford for a postal conference. It was hard to imagine a group of European postal workers convening among Oxford's spires to discern the most effective way to deliver mail from point A to point B. The man asked what we thought of Sicily, and perhaps what Sicilians always ask foreigners, ironically: 'Have you seen any Mafiosi?' His smile suggesting that this was their bogey man, this was how they titillated the tourists.

V.

When we finally reached Palermo after driving back along the A29 and into the city, it was well after dark. The city on first inspection resembled other Mediterranean cities – Marseilles or Alexandria: wide boulevards, modern apartment blocks and jostled among them a few remaining fin-de-siecle Liberty style villas; major traffic junctions grid locked and populated with gleaming Mercedes next to incessantly bleating mopeds, farm trucks and three-wheeled buggies. After getting lost for a while and driving around following his intuition Martin arrived miraculously outside Paolo's modern apartment building in the new city.

Aithne had dated Paolo when she had lived in Palermo, ten years previously. That was when he was a youthful Adonis, with long curly golden locks, piercing blue eyes and an impish grin. He had visited Martin and Aithne several times in London, and over the course of their relationship they had witnessed a decline in his ability to deal with people and a general growing misanthropy. It manifested itself and was partly caused by his relationship with Francesca, his long time off-and-on girlfriend with whom Martin and Aithne were also on good terms. But it had other origins, which had to do with his being Sicilian.

As a young man who barely made it through college, Paolo had traded off his good looks in a place where good looks really count, to land a job assisting a famous Sicilian photojournalist. This woman specialised in taking pictures of corpses of murdered Mafiosi, and anyone else the Mafia murdered in the course of their business transactions. During the nineteen eighties this proved a very time-consuming job. Between 1981 and 1983, several Mafia families, hitherto acting more or less together in a commissione, began feuding. The Corleonesi, upon which Mario Puzzo based his Godfather series, allied with the Greco and Calo families against the Inzerillo, Spatola and Bontate clans. These struggles plunged Palermo into virtual night-time curfews and kept regular people off the streets for fear of getting in the cross-fire or, possibly worse, becoming witness to a murder. In the space of a few years, there were hundreds of victims of this war; the rate of Mafia deaths in the late 1980s reached three hundred per year. Bodies turned up in town dumpsters, were discovered in cars parked on the street, or, in perhaps the most sinister of cases, simply disappeared without a trace, a method referred to as the *Lupara Bianca* by practitioners – the white shotgun.

After several years of this, Paolo quit, and negotiated one of those life-time Italian jobs, as an archivist for the Commune of Palermo. He worked about thirty hours a week, occasionally documenting a building or a section of the city for posterity. But this job actually arose out of an anti-Mafia sensibility. After the war the Mafia was responsible for the vast majority of construction contracts. Out of 4200 building permits issued in the early sixties most went to five obscure figures acting for Mafia interests. In Palermo this building spree resulted in the pulling down of many old palazzi and the erection of cheap totalitarian housing projects which now characterize so much of the city. Under the present (anti-Mafia) Mayor, Leoluca Orlando, there has been a push for civic pride resulting in a surge of restoration projects, and a new awareness of what Palermo has to offer architecturally and civically.

Unlike many other Sicilian kids in the eighties, Paolo had narrowly avoided the heroin craze (courtesy of the Sicilian Mafia which controlled almost all of the heroin trade to the United States, and which made Sicily the biggest refinery in the world). Heroin had burned through a whole generation of Palermitani like an airborne virus. Italy had one of the highest addiction rates in the world during the nineteen eighties, and was the only country in the world where the primary cause of AIDS was dirty needles. Several of Paolo's friends had died, and his sister had been permanently damaged by her habit. As for Paolo, although he had escaped addiction, seeing him now and getting to know him for a few days made me question how much he had escaped, both his Sicilian upbringing and the general trauma of a heroin society.

Paolo greeted us with a reserved warmth, in a pair of baggy work pants and a sweatshirt. His apartment was owned by his parents who lived upstairs, but whom Martin and Aithne, with twelve-odd trips to Palermo over the years, had met only once or twice in the hallway. Soon after our arrival he dragged out sheaves of black and white photographs to show us. His bony thirty five-year-old body bent over the prints carefully. These were all documentary in one form or another, some from Marseilles where he had recently been for an exhibition of photographers from around the Mediterranean. As we flipped through this voluminous work Paolo slowly rolled a joint , then stuck it to his bottom lip where it hung precipitously. His photos were street shots in the style of Magnum or some other news photo agency; reflections of people in café windows, gypsies sleeping on the sidewalk, flower sellers, a pigeon on a medieval lintel.

Then he showed us what had been his magnum opus, several years ago now but a legacy off of which he was still trading. He had documented the ritual processions surrounding *I morti*, the Sicilian day of the dead. These included shots of nuns staring across hilltop villages; old men hauling rough-hewn wooden crosses down narrow alleys; women wailing in grief on the sides of the roads; men wearing devil masks, gyrating in the streets of Prizzi. One showed up close several elderly pairs of hands clutching rosary beads, behind them a hillside gave way to a huge vista of the Sicilian countryside, darkened by cloud. Many of these photos were beautiful, capturing the otherworldliness of the events and possessing their own aesthetic merits. And they all talked about how spirituality was etched into the landscape of Sicily. For Paolo death was a major preoccupation of Sicily, and in that respect this work was related to his Mafia work.

While Paolo was interested in the many faces of Sicilian death, he was also interested in the pre-Christian vestiges of these ritual celebrations. The idea of death and rebirth seemed to link pre-Christian with Christian Sicily. Much has been written about Sicily's Catholicism, and much of it focuses on the continuation of older, Hellenistic influences, such as the cult of Demeter. Pulling on his joint, by now settled under a tall red-velvet lampshade in his old leather armchair, Paolo didn't look much like a professor; he talked in stumbling English about how Sicily was locked into ancient pre-Christian religion. Demeter, the goddess who is supposed to have bestowed agriculture on humanity, was said to have resided at Enna, the central Sicilian town perched high on a rock overlooking the island's cereal plains. It was Demeter who lost her daughter, Persephone, to Hades, lord of the underworld, when he kidnapped her from under her mother's watchful gaze. Demeter's loss of her daughter precipitated winter, as her mournful response to loss, and subsequently produced the seasons and the agricultural civilization which depended upon them. 'There is a church in Enna,' Paolo said, 'where, just one or two generations ago, you could find images of

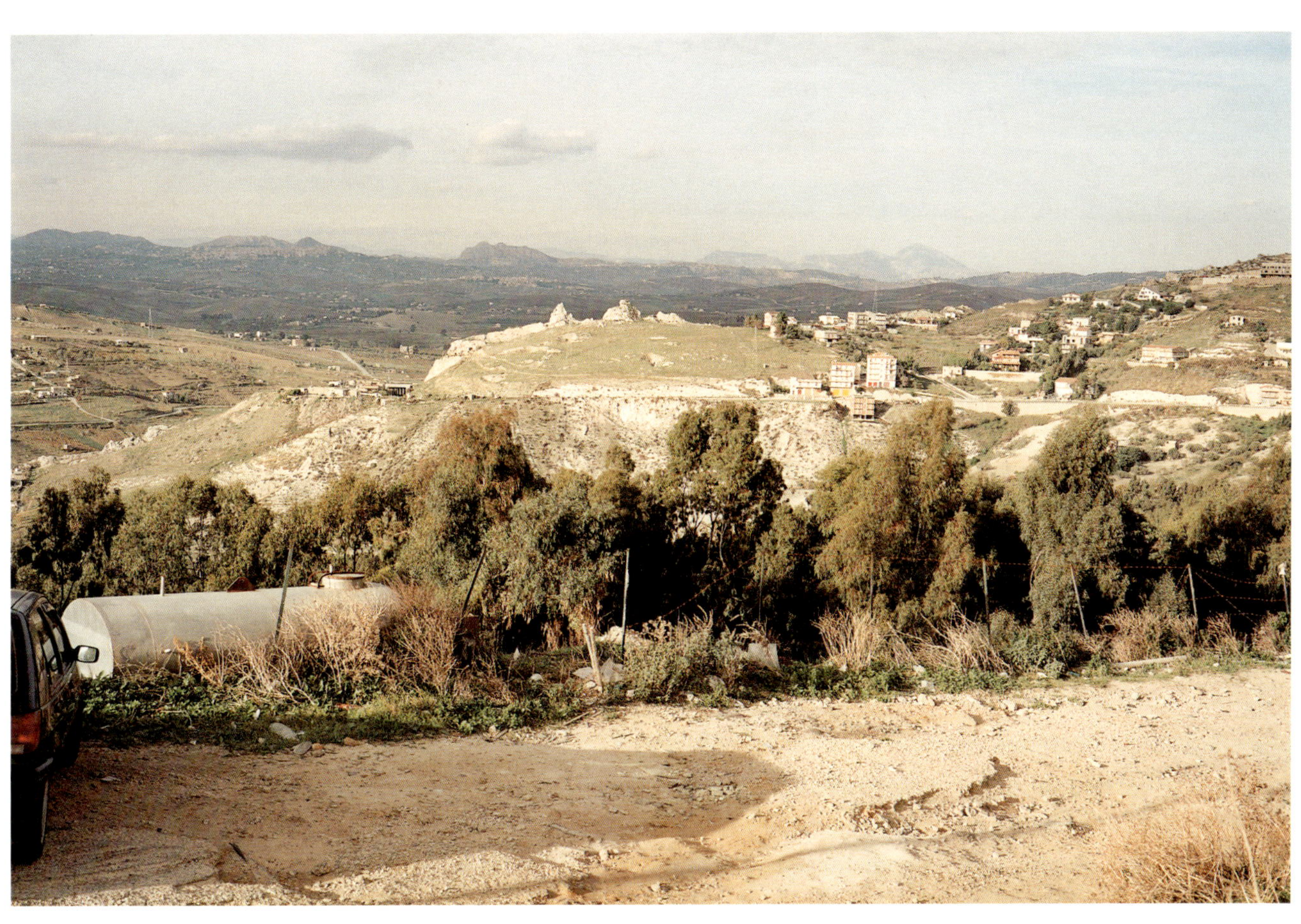

heathen gods and goddesses! Goddess worship, in a Catholic church!'

Reading Raleigh Trevelyan later that night, he also seemed to think that you did not need to look far to discover the past lurking in the guise of the present: 'The more one travels around the island, the more one begins to suspect that the archaic and classical divinities have never quite lost their hold… At Erice, mysterious and silent, I was not surprised to find two people making love on the site of the temple of Venus.' Trevelyan lists many other examples of Sicily's sense of continuity: for example the Devil Dancers of Prizzi, their origins lost in pre-history, and in Agrigento, on the south coast, the annual Almond Blossom festivities celebrate spring, and essentially Persephone's seasonal return from Hades. The figure of the Madonna herself evokes images of the earlier Demeter whose child is lost to death. The wailing women following the procession of the cross in the Easter celebrations are, therefore, reminiscent of Demeter's grief over Persephone, perhaps as much as Mary's over Jesus.

Paolo took us out to eat, although it was late, and although he was accustomed to eating with his parents upstairs. Martin had told me of the delights of Sicilian cuisine, and of how it left the rest of Italian food far behind. Paolo however was not much for eating. We went into the old part of Palermo, which is a rabbit-warren of slim alleys, dark corners and the occasional towering villa or church with wide piazzas opening up. In a small grubby square that was completely devoid of people, Paolo found the pizzeria he was looking for.

He talked a little more about his recent exhibition in Marseilles, and about his need to get away from Sicily; he sounded self-obsessed and maundering and I was more concerned to be enjoying this first Sicilian meal. The same people, he said, were always creating lethargy in Palermo. He was talking of politicians and corrupt local officials who make innovation impossible. Walking around the neighbourhood after dinner he pointed out a poster advertising an artist who had come to Palermo for a showing of his latest documentary film, which Paolo had seen: 'But usually there's nothing going on here. That's why I go to everything there is. We have to get what we can'. We walked for a while through more deserted neighbourhoods in the old city, then through the silent streets of the Vucchiria, the central market, which during the day is bustling and full of extraordinary fresh produce and has all the makings of an oriental bazaar. But now all the carts were shut up and shops closed.

We came into one piazza ringed by ruined houses, the result of bomb damage inflicted in the Second World War when the allies had softened up Palermo before their invasion. It was like going back in time fifty years: these houses had never been restored. As far as I could tell they looked just as they had immediately after the bombs fell. Some groups of artists, however, had taken them on as projects and painted murals over their craggy walls, and in one case where the exterior wall of a house was missing, they had painted wallpaper and inserted a couple of armchairs and a table on the floor. From this position inhabitants of the house could sit and watch the goings on in the piazza.

For all of his apparent dyspepsia, Paolo was involved in the city and its concerns, and was clearly not alone in this among young people, who felt connected to the rest of Europe, tired with Sicily's geographical and cultural isolation, and impatient with the state's endemic corruption. We drove to an ice-cream parlor that Paolo chose. Martin had his own ideas about where the good

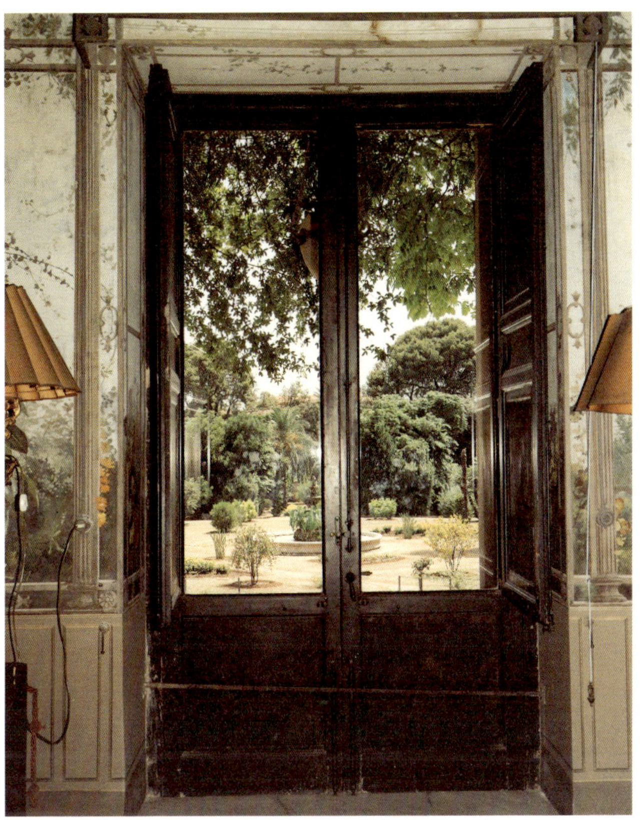

ice cream was to be found but let Paolo call the shots. We pulled up next to a small stand on the road behind which were a few chairs and tables. A handful of young Palermitani were sitting eating brioche filled with ice cream and chatting on mobile phones. This was the first sign of life we had seen in the city so far. Paolo recommended a special kind of nutty ice cream that he claimed was 'healthy', as it was mostly ground up nuts. Martin issued noises of disapproval and avoided his advice, then he started talking about the sexual symbolism of how they eat ice cream in Sicily.

A brioche is a small bun of soft, absorbent bread; it is cut open in the middle and a couple of large scoops are inserted. To eat the ice cream you need to pass your tongue along the edge of the ice cream, which protrudes slightly from the two sides of the bread. As you consume, the ice cream retreats into its bready vagina, and the tongue is forced to follow it. Eating in general is quite closely associated with sex, the resemblance being the bringing of foreign elements inside the body. The boundaries between internal and external are permeated. But it is rare that you are forced to eat something in a way that actually apes a sexual act. The banana comes to mind. Which leads us to the cone: having the brioche and the cone available as options for ice cream consumption leads to some difficult choices if you are sensitive to the symbolism of these vehicles. And it's not surprising to find such sexual symbolism accompanying ice-cream, an inherently sensual food. I looked around at the young people eating ice-cream next to us. Most of the men had their tongues deep inside their brioche, while most of the women were busily licking cones. A few people had chosen a third way: the cup.

VI.

In the morning we found that Paolo had left for work at the archives. We sauntered across the street to a café where we stood and ordered cappuccino and ricotta-filled croissants. The breakfast rush was fast and furious, with the neatly uniformed bar-staff producing oceans of coffee at a staggering pace. Martin warned me about being too friendly or even polite: 'It doesn't suit the macho ethic here to say thank you. All you say is due caffé, no please, no thank you, otherwise they'll think you're some kind of homosexual.' I looked around the bar and listened to other people ordering and noticed a certain lack of politesse. This kind of macho, surly culture had to be associated with rural, and in particular, mountain life where the struggle for existence had always been a hard one. Palermo, which had long been a sophisticated urban centre, was constantly being infiltrated by people from the countryside, especially this century when peasants left their mountain fastnesses in search of a better and easier life in town. And for us, a couple of strange men, adopting the right attitude in the café context was important to avoid any lack of respect. Surviving here, it seemed, required a different conception of what it was to be a man. I remembered Vito Corleone's pithy statements on the issue presented through Marlon Brando and his mouth full of cotton wool: 'A man who doesn't spend time with his family is not a real man'. Interestingly Mario Puzzo presented a Mafia world in which the family was paramount. In fact his novel was about family more than about crime, family being the raison d'etre of the Sicilian 'man of honour'. Here in this café atmosphere there seemed to be a governing ethic of lone, single men, tough and inscrutable. 'And don't smile at anyone', Martin added, as I struggled with an urge to be friendly.

We spent a couple of days in Paolo's apartment. He was at work during the morning and came home in the early afternoon. He seemed to eat lunch and dinner with his parents, so he wasn't around much for eating with us. Often when we came back to the apartment he would appear on the stairs, coming down from his parents apartment with a bundle of clean laundry. This was about as close as you can get to living with your parents without actually co-habiting, and it was absolutely normal for young and not-so-young Palermitani. Paolo's on-and-off girlfriend, Francesca, was in the same situation. We had to be careful how we talked about her in front of Paolo. Once or twice in the last couple of years, Paolo had lost it in front of Martin and Aithne over this subject. They had been a couple for ten or more years, but the last three or four had seen a major evolution in their relationship. They still had the same friends, a close circle, and spent most of their time avoiding each other, which is very difficult in Palermo. Paolo had exhibited extreme jealousy, 'a kind of archetypal Mediterranean honour thing', Martin called it, having to do with possession over women. Reading Norman Lewis in Paolo's spare bedroom, I found an anecdote which reminded me of Paolo's situation. It concerned Don Calogero Vizzini, the Mafia don whom the Allies appointed mayor of Villalba after the war (thus positioning the Mafia to control all of Sicily once more).

In his youth Don Calogero had a crush on a young woman, although for unclear reasons did not follow up on it. When an outsider came to woo her, he gathered a group of thugs together, and beat him up so badly that the woman in question, a beautiful, intelligent girl, was single for the rest of her life as no one would go near her out of fear thereafter. Don Calogero failed to make an honest woman of her and instead condemned her through his action to die as a spinster.

Francesca wasn't taking any of Paolo's possession crap, however. She was doing her own thing and seeing other people, apparently considering their relationship over. This all meant that Martin and I had to be very circumspect when talking to Francesca and arranging to see her, for fear of upsetting Paolo.

When we did finally meet up with her, at her parents' apartment where she was living, she was recovering from some sort of gynecological surgery. Her parents lived in a penthouse suite of a very tall building in the new part of Palermo. From the balcony you could see most of the Conco D'oro, a great valley (literally a bowl of gold) that runs into the north-eastern side of the city. The countless orange groves that once carpeted this area replaced by high-rise. Also from this vantage point you could see why the Ancient Greeks called it Panormus – 'all harbour'. The land swoops round in a huge encompassing claw, protected on three sides with the mountains rising up behind it. From the balcony you could also see the extent of Palermo's massive urban sprawl. High-rise blocks stretched way up into the hills, with several extensive new developments eating their way up increasingly steep mountain-sides. According to the writer Peter Robb, Italy has for decades consumed more concrete per capita than any country in the world. One of these developments, Francesca pointed out, was a prime example of the construction industry in Palermo. Mafia Hill, as it was known locally, boasted dozens of new villas built into the hillside looking over the wealthy resort of Mondello, just down the coast from Palermo proper. The hillside had been cleared, bulldozed, and a dirt road had been scraped, zigzagged against the mountain's face. This construction was in direct contradiction to the city's zoning laws and planning, but typically, according to Francesca, this had been overlooked. But the fate of Mafia Hill was now in question, and looking at it, it was clear that work had stopped some time ago, although some hefty mortgages had already been taken out against these unfinished villas.

We sat and had coffee in Francesca's parents' living room. I was beginning to understand how easy it must be, travelling here and meeting people, to see the hand of the Mafia in almost everything: behind every successful doctor, in every union action, in the movement of farm goods in and out of the city.

On the walls were reproduction Monets and Manets and a few other heavily-framed oil paintings. Francesca was a gracious hostess, elegant and courteous, in stark contrast to Paolo's hermit-like, somewhat misanthropic personality. She sat looking slightly uncomfortable, still in a little pain after her surgery, draped in a cotton shawl like an old lady. She apologised for her bad English, although it was very good, and we conversed in our bad Italian, a little French and English mixed together. Francesca actually taught French at a local school whenever they needed her, and was trying to negotiate a full-time permanent position. If she succeeded the job would be hers pretty much for life. This was the kind of deal Paolo had with the city and clearly it was the most desirable situation, providing life-long stability. Francesca brought up the fact of her living with her parents, and joked about Palermitans not being mentally able to leave home, but the truth being that family life is important in Sicily, and it is not seen as aberrant to live with your parents until you are married. The notion of living alone 'like they do in the United States' was horrific and unrealistic to her. There was some additional poignancy in

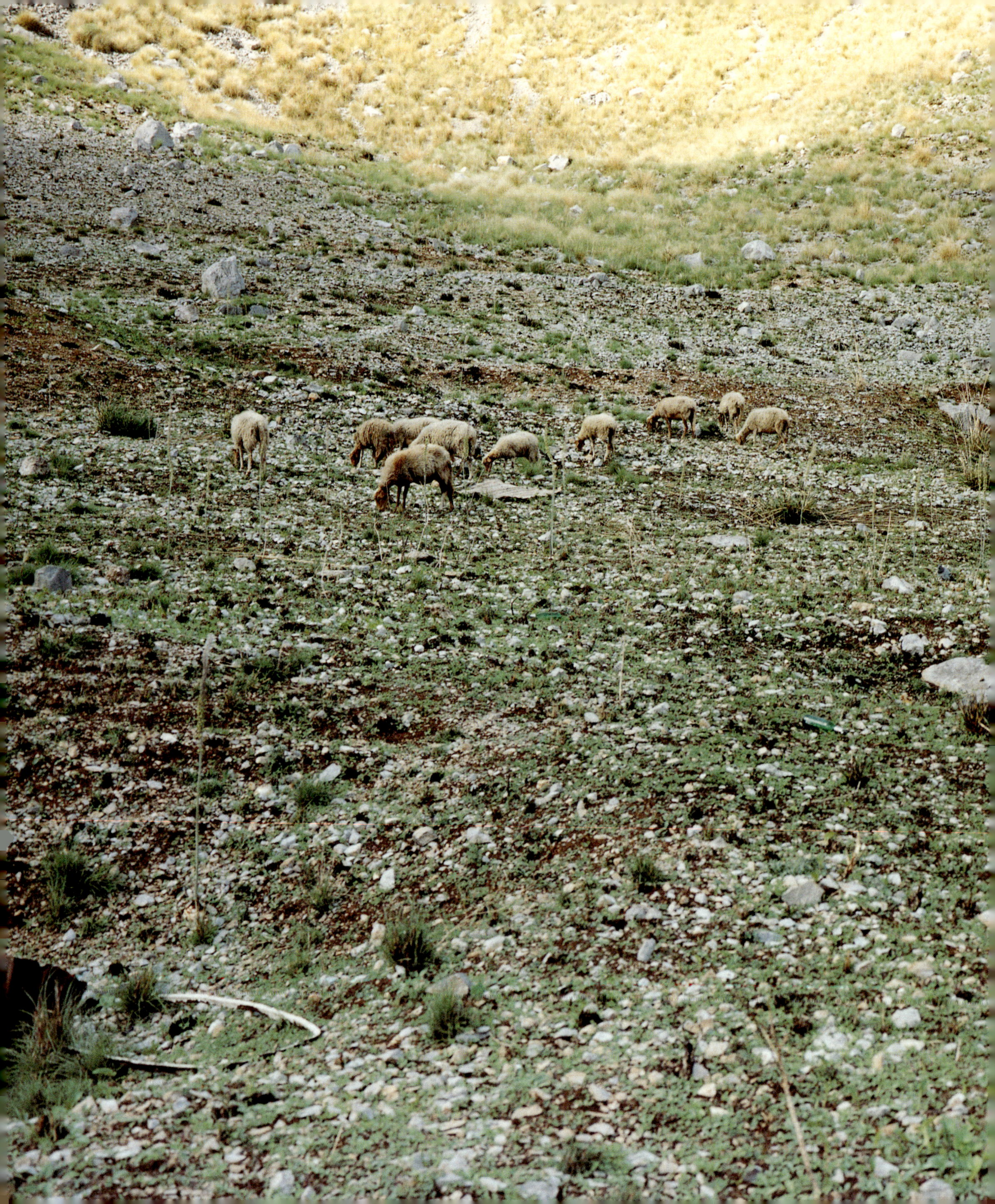

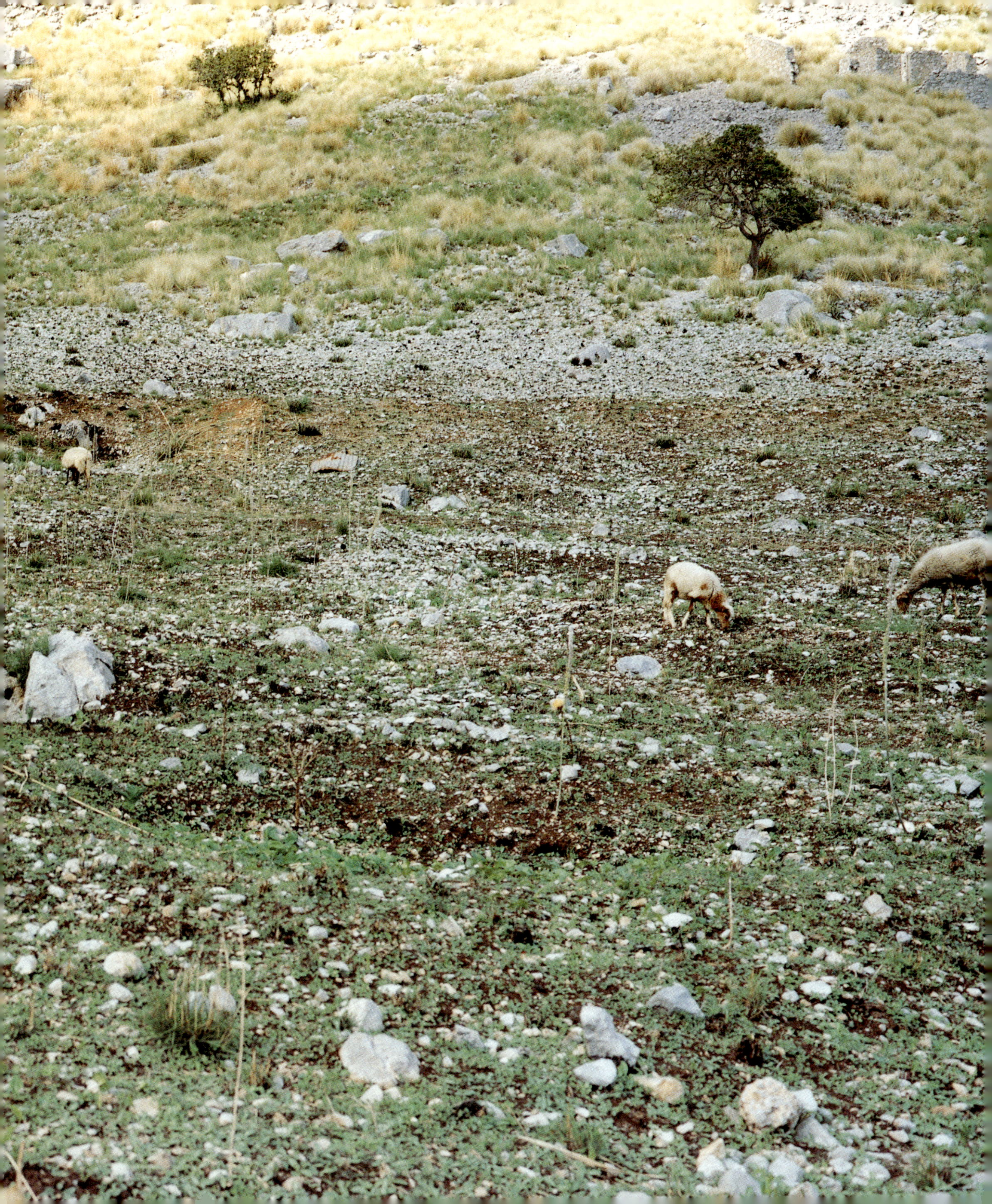

her description of family-oriented culture and the question of marriage because of her failed relationship with Paolo. These two professional people, both from middle-class, comfortable families, yet living alone in the home-stretch to middle age that is the mid-thirties.

When we returned to Paolo's he was in his dark room with a joint firmly planted between his teeth. He wandered around the apartment muttering to himself, and then casually mentioned that there was a gasoline strike, and he had spent all day driving around town looking for fuel, unsuccessfully. We listened to this in horror, as we were planning to drive two hundred miles the next day, across the island. He knew of our plans, and as Martin cross-questioned him it dawned on me that he was absolutely resigned about the prospect of several days (maybe weeks – who knew?) of immobility.

VII.

'This landscape, which knows no mean between sensuous sag and hellish drought; which is never petty, never ordinary, never relaxed, as a country made for rational beings to live in should be.'

So says the Prince in Giuseppe Di Lampedusa's famous novel *The Leopard*. Almost everyone writing on Sicily must deal, in addition to the Mafia, with Lampedusa, if only to reference him. Although almost without plot, his only novel is extraordinarily compelling and highly evocative in its creation of a sense of place and the place's effect on the characters. The Prince speaks like a personification of Sicily itself; decadent, defiant, morose, meditative and, at times, harsh. And his appreciation of the Sicilian landscape is central to his understanding of Sicilians and Sicily's political past and future. Lampedusa's characters are in some way formed by the Sicilian landscape, just as the landscape informs the island's history. It was these relationships that Martin was intent on observing through his camera on his way across the island.

The next morning we left early. On leaving the apartment we shouted goodbye to Paolo. The night before we had gone out looking for fuel. We found long lines at the pumps, but a little diesel. Paolo had been remarkably uninterested, which infuriated Martin who sensed that, as a host, Paolo should have been more proactive. We received a monosyllabic response from his darkened bedroom, like the ones Lampedusa referred to as 'the guttural emissions which Sicilians use in anger'. We left Palermo to drive through the landscape so well captured by Lampedusa, through the plains of central Sicily, through the Madonie mountains of the north and the coast near Messina where the Norman knight, Roger, had first entered Sicily on his conquering crusade. As we drove along the

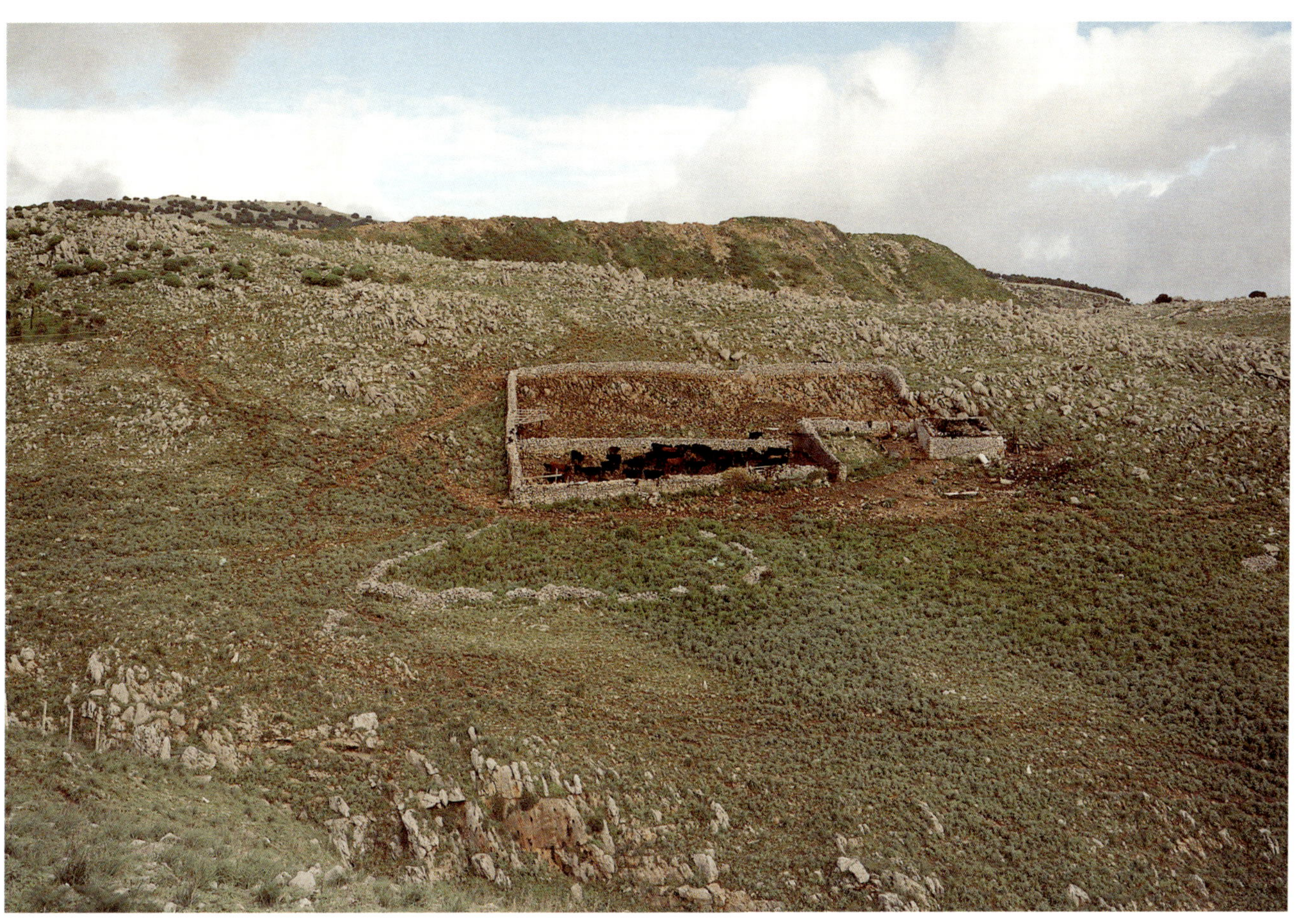

coast for a while, we looked at the patches of agricultural activity taking place by the shore, mostly olive trees. Then we turned south and towards the centre of the island. Here the valleys were deeper and along their sides were terraces full of dark green lemon trees. I was surprised at how lush these valleys were, and before long I was surprised, too, at the rolling plains we encountered which were so well hidden from the coast. Goethe had also been surprised by these plains. Although Sicily has been a bread basket for centuries, if you do not go into the interior, the impression one has of the island is of mountains and valleys with agriculture possible only in small intensive enclaves: 'Wherever the soil is suitable to (wheat and barley's) growth, it is so well tended and exploited that not a tree is to be seen. Even the small hamlets and other dwellings are confined to the ridges.'

The road of which Goethe did not have the benefit in the 1780s cuts through these 'gently rolling uplands'. It afforded us an incredible range of positions from which to view the scenery. In fact the highway seemed to have been built with an appreciation of its place in the landscape, so that its majestic sweep and curve was not incongruous with the movements of the earth on which it was laid. Tall pillars carried it over the deep gorges that sometimes accommodated flashfloods, the like of which would carry away so fragile a piece of engineering as a highway. Cuts and embankments did not appear too numerous, and although the road seemed to continue its gentle progression east-west, uninhibited by steep and sudden inclines, it remained true to the natural lay of the land. It followed the path of least resistance in circum-navigating outcroppings, sliding between hillsides, skirting or jumping ravines.

We got out of the car and stood facing the sweep of the gigantic fields up to the horizon. The highway was in fact practically empty, and for some moments we were alone in this huge space without even a trace of a town or hamlet. There were, however, a few small dwellings noticeable on the hillsides. These were the Pagliarini, which Goethe also mentioned, the shepherds huts. In discussing the relationship between the Mafia and petty crime, Norman Lewis talks about thieves, a kind of untouchable caste, that occasionally rob these huts. They are, he says, 'hunted down like dogs', and killed by the Mafia. But the rural villages and towns have historically been pretty much empty of men in the summer, when the animals are taken up to the higher pastures for weeks on end. 'Historically' here, meaning for centuries, and still, to some extent, today. The old men, old before their time, hobbling about Sicilian towns today with bandy legs and weather-beaten skins, are the last real generation of peasants; their children are likely to be found in towns holding down less strenuous occupations, if they are lucky.

Since open countryside was a dangerous place to be because of bandits well into the nineteen seventies, Sicilians huddled together in towns often miles from the fields that the men worked. This necessitated early risings, long walks to work and long returns on foot. The Mediterranean historian, Fernand Braudel, makes much of mountain civilizations and their severity: 'In the mountains, society, civilization and economy all bear the marks of backwardness and poverty.' This is true almost wherever mountains play a part around the Mediterranean. But this mountain society was not poor just because of its mountains: Sicily's peasant poverty came from centuries of absentee-landlordism and the exploitation of both the resources of the island and its peasant population. Sicily, as many historians have pointed out, has been doomed to eternal domination by outsiders: Greeks, Arabs, Normans, Germans, Spanish, English, and finally, Italians. According to the historian Moses Finley: 'It is impossible to calculate how much produce and money has been taken out of Sicily in rents, taxes, and plain looting in the past two thousand years.' As a bread basket of Rome there was little left to feed the local producers of this bread. And it was the condition of absentee-landlordism which greatly helped the development of the Mafia. The landlords sold leases, often very badly, to local bosses who, as short term lease holders, worked the peasants to the maximum and extracted the maximum from them in terms of taxes, not thinking in the long-term interest of the estate, the land and the peasantry, but of short-term gain. These Mafia middle-men started out working for the noble class and ended up displacing them altogether.

Driving by these fields of wheat and barley, recently harvested, it was disquieting to imagine the inexhaustable ocean of wealth they represented to tiny groups of people, far away, and in direct relation the wretched lives of those who worked them. To Martin, these wheat-producing plains, famous in antiquity and all but forgotten today, were like an historical text, lying in nature's archives to be read by some studious academic.

VIII.

We stayed on the East Coast in the town of Acireale, in a large hotel with the upbeat name of the Aloha Dora. The hotel was on the main coastal road which is perched high up above the sea in classic Mediterranean style. Behind the hotel, in the distance, loomed the massive, cloud covered summit of Mount Etna, Europe's largest active volcano. Made almost exclusively from black aerated lava stone, and whitewashed in places, the hotel occupied several terraces above the sea, which spread out before it in a huge swell towards the Straits of Messina and the rugged Mezzogiorno of Italy's mainland. As we checked into the hotel we noticed a large bulletin board in the lobby announcing a 'congress' of Italian policeman. The theme was 'The New Technology in the Service of Fighting Crime'. Our hotel seemed to be where the Italian state had gathered to examine how the Internet in another part of its world-improving mission was going to end the rule of the Italian mob. We joked about bustthemob.gov, hitman.com and protectionracket.org, (this one being a non-profit outfit to train start-up Mafiosi). A couple of days later we saw in the Giornale Di Sicilia, an article about a member of the organised crime underground who had swindled local banks out of millions via the Internet. Clearly the mob had already enjoyed their own congress: 'The New Technology in the Service of Organised Crime'.

Other guests included a large group of German tourists who had recently arrived in a bus and were busy finding passports and negotiating who was going to sleep where. Having completed the check-in Martin was keen to explore some of the *thermae* we had seen advertised on the road as we entered town, so we set off again down the coast road. The *thermae* in Acireale were worlds away from the hidden, breize-block building in which we had swum on the first night in Sicily. These were great nineteenth-century palazzi, places to go for the cure, where foreigners and Italians alike would have come from afar to 'take the waters'. We went into the largest of these establishments perched on a hillside overlooking the coast road and found it full of elderly people and staff in white coats. We were directed to a ticket office where, having consulted a lengthy menu of options, we paid for the basic sulphur bath.

In order to receive the treatment we had to make our way to another building across the road, overlooking the sea. There was a bus already laid on to transport us the several hundred yards, but when we witnessed it being loaded with other 'patients' well into their eighties, and most of them apparently unable to walk, we decided we should take our own transportation. While in Italy there is a massive state whose officials are ever-present, this does not translate into increased efficiency. We experienced the reality of the Italian employment policy when we arrived at the bathhouse in our car; here we were greeted by a fat middle aged man in a sweat suit and a T-shirt, brandishing a whistle. While it was blindingly obvious where we should park, this attendant gesticulated, blew his whistle, grinned and motioned towards the spot as we manoeuvered the car into it. It was not easy to see how this activity would have been more difficult without him there. This wasn't the first time I'd noticed superfluous parking attendants; almost anywhere where there are more than four or five spaces in Sicily you can find someone like this. People studiously ignore them, although it is considered impolite to not disburse the requisite five hundred lire piece for services rendered. While this phenomenon is a logical extension of an over-employed state, it is also in Sicily part of the protection-racket society. In the relationship between motorist and attendant is the mutual awareness of superfluity, but a tacit agreement to overlook it, and this involves something vaguely threatening: 'I am performing a useless service, but go ahead and try to avoid paying me for it'.

Whereas the parking area was awash with unnecessary help, there was no one obviously ready to welcome us inside. Having spent a few minutes wandering around the huge lobby, looking at elderly people wandering as aimlessly as us, we eventually noticed a group of young women sitting at a desk chatting. Since they seemed the most official sight around, we lingered in front of them until one of them noticed us and asked us if she could help. We presented our receipt from the office where we had paid and this unleashed a flurry of confusion, bordering on panic, among the several women at the desk, as if they had been given orders from the Prime Minister to shut the place down in the next hour. After walking up and down some corridors, we were told to sit down outside an office with the word 'Acqua' on the door, so we sat down and watched the young woman disappear.

After a few minutes Martin's need for customer service and his suspicion of Sicilian *laissez faire* propelled him back towards the desk with the young women, who, on seeing him approaching, were thrown once again into hysteria. He was reassured that someone would be with him and then told that we first needed to have or medical examination. This was more than we had bargained for and we tried to explain that we just wanted a hydrological massage and some sulphurous treatment, as if this was the most normal thing in the world. After a few more garbled interactions an elegantly-dressed female doctor walked into the lobby and was

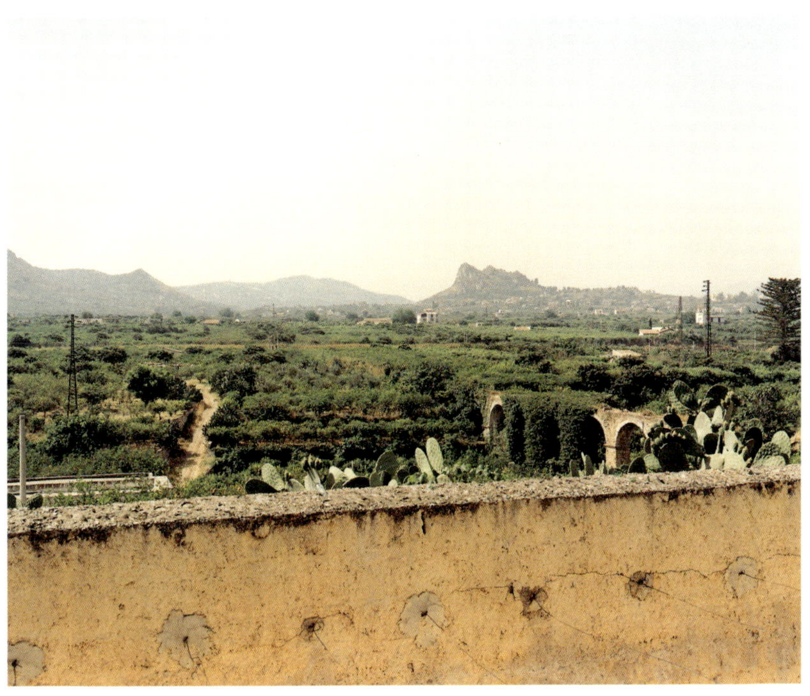

immediately surrounded by elderly supplicants to whom she spoke softly and issued palliative assurances which mostly involved the repetition of the word *domani*. For whatever reason she didn't say *domani* to us when our assistant gave her our papers and explained the situation. We were ushered into her office where she adopted a business-like attitude and rolled up our sleeves. Some people, she explained, have high blood pressure, which is dangerous in situations of extreme heat. We were swiftly examined, found fit to proceed to the next stage, and subsequently led out of the office.

The upstairs was indeed like a hospital – sterile and white. We found ourselves divided; I was taken into a small room where the hydrology treatment was conducted. A small chubby man in overalls invited me to undress and then left to run the bath: in the next room, a grubby plastic tub with two taps on one end. Around the taps some sort of green algae was accumulating. The bath was frothing alarmingly with greenish, stinking bubbles, and the small chubby man reappeared and invited me into the fetid tub. Once immersed, small jets were activated which propelled the stinking water at my body. The man left me to enjoy my hydrological massage and disappeared for half an hour. I lay back gently boiling in this froth, thinking that this was not quite what we had been after, but that it was probably very relaxing, and I wondered whether they had many young foreigners here without any particular ailments. When the chubby assistant re-appeared he tested the water with his hand and squinted intently at something behind me and above my head, which I assumed was a clock (although on turning around there was nothing but a bare wall). When he motioned for me to get out I was quite relieved, but not for long.

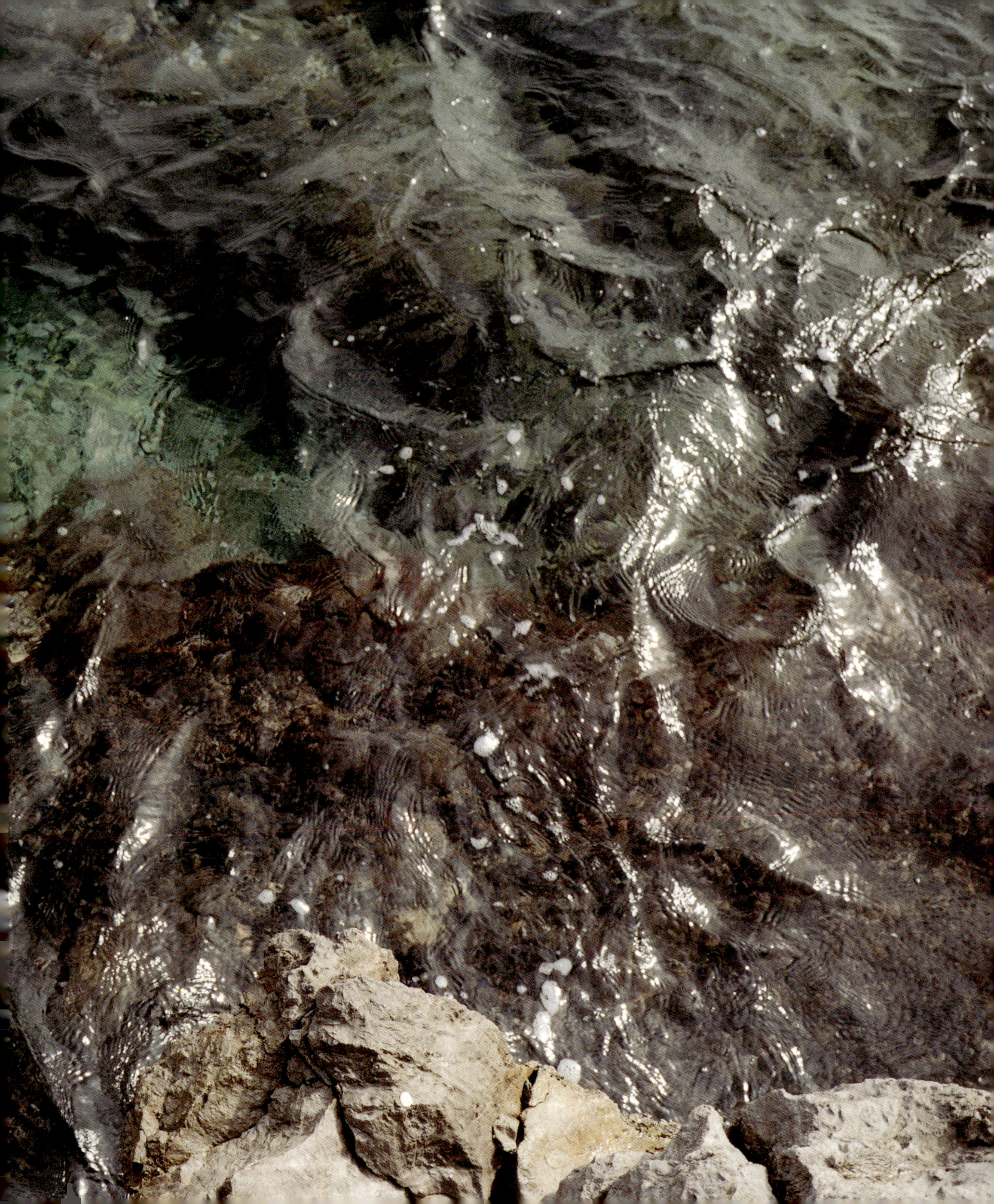

He showed me into a room with a bed and wrapped me in a cotton sheet. This was a little uncomfortable. Then I was told to lie on the bed whereupon he wrapped me like a mummy in a voluminous sheet of plastic, and over that added a thick wool blanket. I watched in horror as these new layers were applied and felt my temperature increase alarmingly. As much as I had brought this treatment upon myself and was partly convinced of its beneficial effects, I doubted how long I could tolerate such heat. I asked the man how long this would take and he responded with a non-committal 'not long', and I realised that the culture of this overridingly medical establishment was authoritarian, and profoundly at odds with my understanding of holistic health. The sulphur, he told me, needed to get absorbed into the skin. Even my head was covered so there was nowhere for the heat to escape. I tried in vain to wriggle at least my toes free so some air could enter my broiling sarcophagus. After five or six minutes the man re-emerged to ensure no air leaks had developed in the system; when he left I felt the simultaneous sensations of claustrophobia and overheating building unbearably, and I thought of that experiment in which subjects are told by men in white coats to press switches which trigger screams of pain from people somewhere else, and wondered whether I should just end this foolishness, now. Finally, after a good twenty-five minutes, the man came back and allowed to me wriggle myself off the bed and peel off the clothes to reveal a truly diabolical stench of sulphur and sweat. He said I could get dressed, and when I asked for a cold shower he was horrified, and launched into a vehement lecture about the benefits of the sulphur and the necessity of its penetrating. The shower, he said, could wait until I got back to my hotel.

Outside in the fresh air, I walked up and down the road, trailed by noxious vapors seeping through my shirt. It felt extraordinarily good to be outside looking at the swell of the Mediterranean two hundred feet below the hillside, and thinking about my close encounter with asphyxiation. Elderly people were hobbling around also, taking the air, after a no doubt equally gruelling experience from which they seemed miraculously to have survived. Soon I spotted Martin reeling out of the building, with his hair standing on end and a glazed expression on his face. We both headed for the car. Out of the corner of my eye I saw the parking attendant inserting his whistle into his mouth, and begin to blow a series of high-pitched, official notes signalling to us that we should not panic, that professional help was on the way to help us exit our parking spot in the most efficient manner possible.

That night we went in search of a culinary experience. We had been in Sicily several days and had not had a notable meal. We'd had some good coffee and some excellent pastries, but had gone light on lunches and had bombed at dinner. We drove along the coast until we found a small fishing village called Capo Mulini, a small collection of houses around a tiny beach and a boat slip. Among the houses there was a disproportionate number of restaurants, suggesting that this was probably a resort for Sicilian tourists. They all served roughly the same menu, a collection of seafood and a small number of pastas, with one or two *anti-pasti*. We walked into one of the more expensive looking establishments and asked if we could see their menu. The waiter who, as Martin pointed out, looked like another Mel Gibson, regarded us severely and handed us the menu with something like disdain. Having assessed it, we made non-committal noises and wandered around the town to check out the competition. Martin was still thinking about the Gibson clone: 'Gibson is Australian, and there are thousands of southern Italians who emigrated to Australia in the nineteenth and early twentieth centuries. It's amazing, in fact in Sicily you often see three primary characters, Mel Gibson, Al Pacino and Robert De Niro, all from Southern Italian stock'.

Eventually we decided that the best bet was the restaurant we had originally gone into to see the menu, and when we returned Mel Gibson was there to greet us (along with another waiter who I thought looked like Woody Allen). Allen, as it turned out, was our waiter, and I had to revise my opinion during the *anti-pasta* because if character determines looks, this guy was distinctly un-Allen-like. He too was extremely sullen and dismissive and we immediately assumed it was because we were foreign and were tapping into some primitive, atavistic dislike of outsiders, or quite possibly we were still being trailed by sulphurous fumes. The breaking point came when in the middle of our *anti-pasta* Allen turned up at the table bearing two hot dishes of pasta. Martin looked at him in surprise and exclaimed, 'but we haven't finished this yet', gesturing at our half-consumed *anti- pasta rustica,* a simple plate of Prosciutto, olives and cheese.

Allen stood swaying in the middle of the room looking at us then looking back at the kitchen, then he turned and marched back the way he had come. Martin glowered after him and started muttering curses under his breath.

'What? So he made a mistake and came to early?' I said.

'No. He did that purposefully to fuck with us. He knew we hadn't finished. What did he expect, we'd just give him our plates, or he'd just dump the stuff on the table before we'd finished?' Martin was boiling with rage, and I realised that whatever Woody had done had touched some long-forgotten nerve in my brother's nervous system, some nerve with Southern Mediterranean connections. Maybe our ancestors emigrated from Sicily too.

'He disrespected us!' Martin said, still glowering alarmingly.

'What!?' I said, amazed at this metamorphosis taking place at the dinner table.

'How do you know he meant to disrespect us?' I thought it would be ill-advised to make a scene here being the only foreigners and in possession of a small armory of Italian words. Martin took a quick look around the room, as if sizing up the occupants. They were quietly getting on with their meals; a family; a young couple; two elderly folks and a middle-aged man by himself. Perhaps this is what had happened when Martin had tried to ram his tiny Lancia through that narrow alleyway in Palermo, becoming impotently and infuriatingly stuck.

'It's a subtle language, but you get used to it eventually. And there's no doubt about it, that was a deliberate snub'. We continued, tensely, to chew on the Prosciutto. Several minutes later Allen was back, all smiles, and when he put down the plates on the table, said with a strangely upbeat perhaps sarcastic tone, 'Okayyy?' Martin stared him down extremely hard, so that the smile disappeared from his face and he turned around sharply and was gone. For the rest of the meal Mel Gibson was our waiter, and performed his duties professionally and with courtesy.

'You see', Martin said, the suspicious glow in his eye diminishing after the fish dish, 'I let him know that he couldn't get away with it and he backed down'. I had to admit, there was something to it. As we left the restaurant later, the manager came running out after us waving a postcard and saying, 'please tell your friends about us!' Suddenly we were the good news ambassadors from Capo Mulini to the great world outside.

The next morning at breakfast we encountered the German group and the Italian police delegation. The crime fighters all looked sleep deprived and a little hung over. As we sat near the espresso bar trying to ensure that the barman was producing the right amount of coffee for us, we watched a huge man with a great square jaw and a very low brow come swaggering into the breakfast room. On either side of him were slightly smaller men dressed, like him, in expensive grey suits. As soon as he approached the bar the barman, who had been busying himself with our coffee, dropped our order and turned his full attention to the big new customer. Martin raised his eyebrow and ordered me under his breath to check out 'The Boss'. The barman was scurrying around assembling the man's order, which I had not witnessed him give. This would have been unremarkable if not for the fact that the same man had been moody and inattentive to us, to the point of rudeness. His attitude had undergone a remarkable adjustment with the entrance of this new customer.

Martin nodded knowingly at the scene, probably the same way he did at Bella Lugosi clones at the airport. This man clearly had more respect capital than a couple of foreigners. I sat wondering, again, at whether Sicily really was so transparent, and whether there was a 'rational' explanation for what appeared to be obeisance being paid to a crime chief. Did the barman recognise this man for what he was, unquestioningly? Were there signs that any Sicilian could read? I remembered an anecdote in Norman Lewis about bandits holding up a bus in the mountains in the nineteen fifties. The bandits lined up the passengers and removed their valuables one by one. When one of the bandits came face to face with one particular man, the man looked him in the eye and said in a tone full of menace, 'You will not touch me'. The bandit paused for a moment then moved on. From that day onwards the town knew of the man's secret affiliation.

IX.

A few days later we were back in Palermo. It was late at night. We had returned with nearly a quarter of a tank of diesel, and were quite pleased with the fuel situation. There was some question of Martin taking me to the airport, however, because Aithne and the baby were to arrive in a few days for a holiday. The porter at Paolo's apartment building greeted us, and asked Martin when the *bambino* was coming out. He and his wife were very excited about Roger. 'I don't know if they would be so attentive if we'd had a girl, though', said Martin.

Paolo was inside his dark cavern of an apartment. Some 70s rock music was playing, Velvet Underground, I think, and he was pottering about. He was his usual luke-warm self, had a glass of wine with us as we ate some take-out dinner, and then announced that he had to go out.

The following morning we had to get up early and meet some friends of Martin who were lending him their villa at Mondello. When we got up we found that Paolo had mysteriously removed our key from its usual place, meaning that we'd have to hope Paolo was home when we returned, and if we missed him we might end up staying out all night while he caroused. Martin was insistent on waking him up: 'We can't just hang around all day waiting for him to show up. He should have thought of leaving a key for us before he went to bed'. He went in and shook Paolo, brushing aside his angry noises of frustration and fatigue. Paolo finally roused himself, slopped across the apartment and found a key, reluctantly giving it to us and announcing that he'd been out until 5am 'dancing in the street'. There was a certain woman involved that had kept him out so late, apparently, and we both wondered later why he hadn't either brought her back here or not returned home at all. Perhaps that was the source of frustration.

'If you're going to spend all night out dancing, then why come back empty handed?' Martin wondered. But Paolo didn't want to discuss anything, and retreated into his room with a banging of doors, a mute fury seeping from his very pores. We left Paolo stewing over his lack of sleep and his inconsiderate house guests and realised it was a very good thing that we would have somewhere else to stay. Something was happening to Paolo that was clearly undermining his ten-year friendship with Martin.

When we came back later that day Paolo was at home. He was conciliatory: 'I'm sorry about my mood this morning. You know, I had no sleep, Saturday's my only day to sleep in, and then after you woke me up all these people called me, Giovanni, Michaela, you know...'.

'You have so many friends, Paolo, they all want to talk to you,' Martin quipped, eliciting a resigned, sad expression from Paolo.

The next week, having left the island, I called Martin at his friend's place in Mondello. I wanted to find out how his family holiday was going. There was a Scirocco blowing, the temperature had soared from the very moderate seventies, which we had experienced, to the oppressive nineties, and the wind, carrying its Saharan cargo, was playing on everyone's nerves. After I had left, and Aithne and Roger had arrived, Paolo had undergone a fit of deep remorse for his surly and anti-social behavior. He had come out to Mondello, his mute presence conveying an apology. Hugs all around had made up for his lapse in social relations and he was back within the fold of society. But now it was Martin who was disgruntled: Sicily, which they had never experienced with a toddler, was an impossible place, and although the Sicilians make such a fuss of children – *i bambini!* – they didn't really know how to accommodate them into everyday life. At restaurants, babies appeared at supremely late hours, neatly primped to be on display. Any expressions of to-be-expected ill-temper were severely admonished, and children were tightly controlled in public spaces, discouraged from running around as they are designed to do. The beach, which looked so inviting from a distance, was full of used condoms, cigarette butts and needles, the detritus of a complex society.

One night outside their villa, which was nestled under a cliff at the end of a private dirt road, a gang of smugglers had unloaded their cargo. Cars and trucks had come and gone all night meeting zodiacs full of cartons. The next morning Carabinieiri Alfa Romeos were everywhere, combing the shoreline; police divers were looking for underwater evidence, the fight against crime in full swing outside their doorway. Meanwhile Signor Tanti, the Mafia shepherd who acted as gate-keeper of the estate and walked around it with a shotgun, was busy in the hills behind the house hunting rabbits. He came into the villa once or twice to fix a plumbing problem, pinching Roger's cheeks on the way out, and rhapsodising over the small boy like a chubby grandmother. Every night, Martin told me, the open, empty ground around the villa was used as an illicit parking lot for amorous couples. Although it was technically a private estate, Signor Tanti accepted gifts from people who wanted to park their car under the cliff for a few hours. Where else could they do what they had to do? In a crowded apartment with grandparents and siblings all over the place?

Having left Sicily it took on a far-away, tragic-comic quality in my imagination. Mondello seemed to be a tiny microcosm containing everything Sicilian, for better or worse. And it seemed to express everything that Martin had for years been excited about in Sicily: 'The Arabs built Scirocco rooms', he often told me, excitedly. 'Imagine: a basement room, water-cooled and dark just for escaping from the extreme temperatures of the season!' Exotica was part of the allure of this idea. But also attractive was the notion of a time in which the climate dictated what we did, where we went, and how we lived; these powers of the natural world having diminished in modernity, and consequently our sense of frail humanity with them.

On the plane back to Rome I had finished Lampedusa's novel and came across this pivotal sentence: 'All Sicilian expression', says the Prince to an envoy of the embryonic Italian state, 'even the most violent, is really wish fulfillment: our sensuality is a hankering for oblivion, our shooting and knifing a hankering for death; our laziness, our spiced sherbets, a hankering for voluptuous immobility, that is, for death again; our meditative air is that of a void waiting to scrutinise the enigmas of nirvana.'

I thought of Paolo, again, emerging from his own void-like apartment and travelling out to Mondello in search of salvation through attachment to human beings, and arriving at the villa, bedraggled and conciliatory, at least for now victorious in this Sicilian dialectic of life and death.

Braudel, Fernand: *The Mediterranean and the Mediterranean World in the Age of Philip II* (London, 1972)
Moses Finley: *Ancient Sicily* (London, 1964)
Goethe: *Italian Journey* (London, 1970)
Giuseppe di Lampedusa: *The Leopard* (New York, 1960)
Norman Lewis: *The Honoured Society* (London,1984)
Norman Lewis: *In Sicily* (London, 2000)
Alta Macadam: *Blue Guide: Sicily* (London, 1999)
Peter Robb: *Midnight in Sicily* (New York, 1996)
Sammartino and Roberts: *Sicily, an Informal History* (New York, 1992)
Mary Taylor Simtei: *On Persephone's Island, A Sicilian Journal* (New York, 1986)
Raleigh Trevelyan: *The Companion Guide to Sicily* (Woodbridge, 1998)

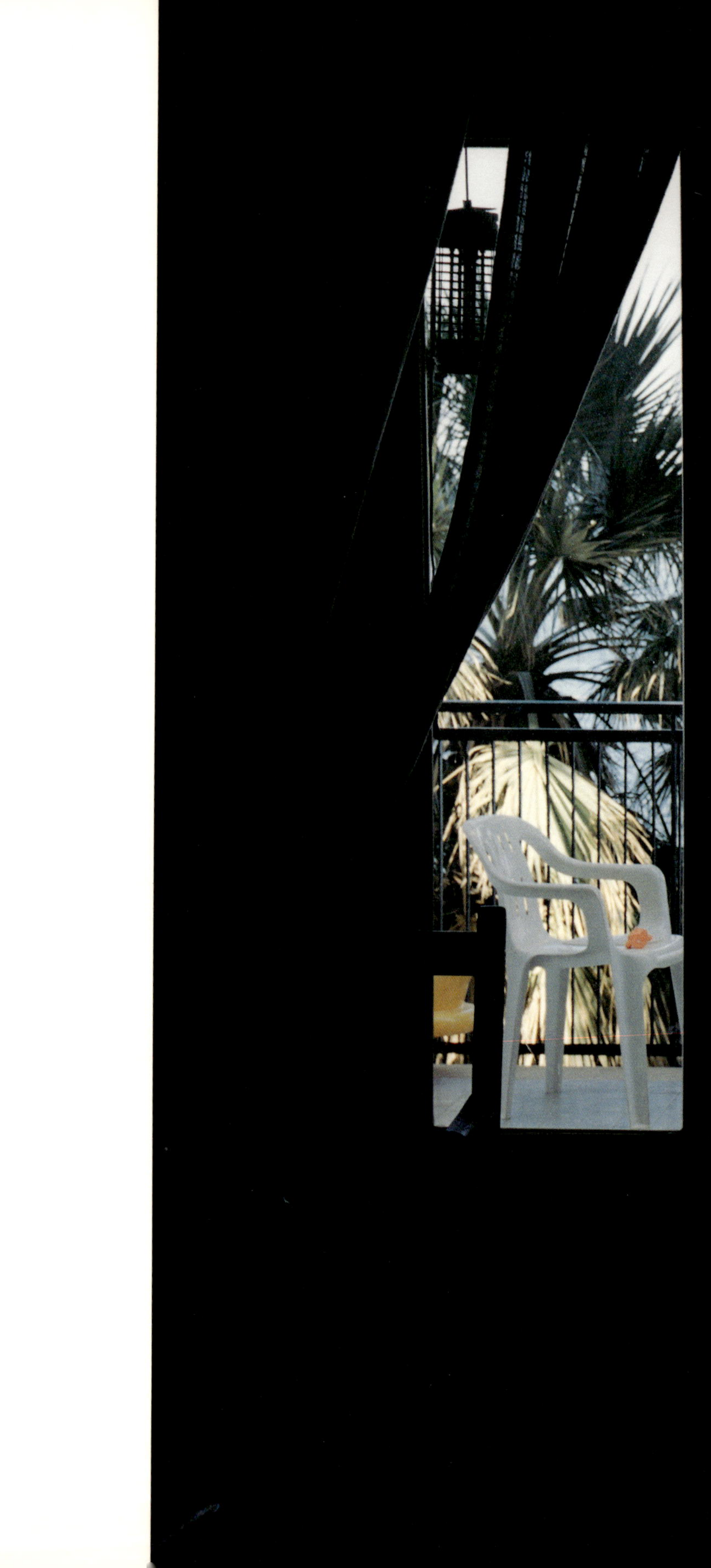

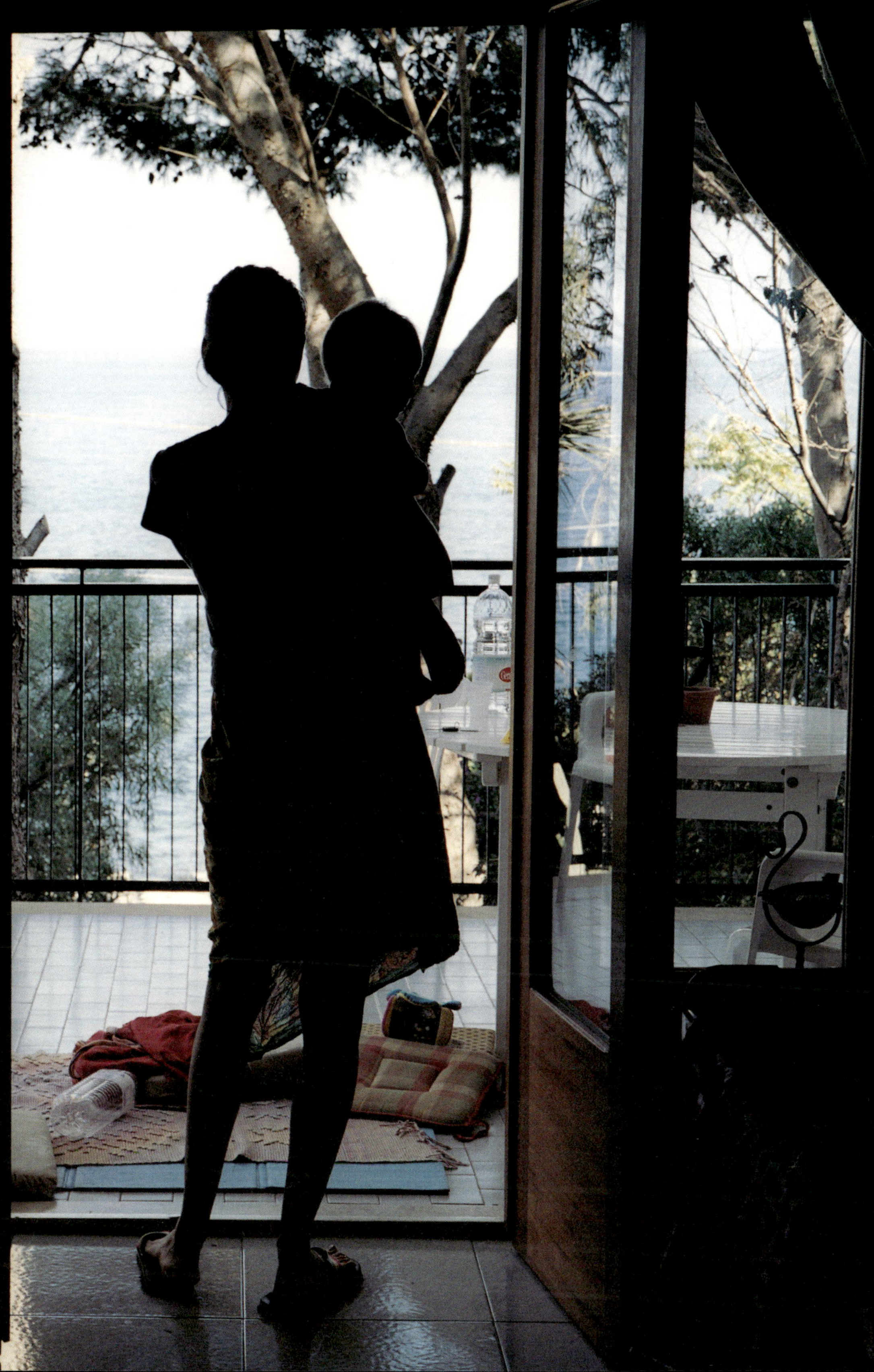

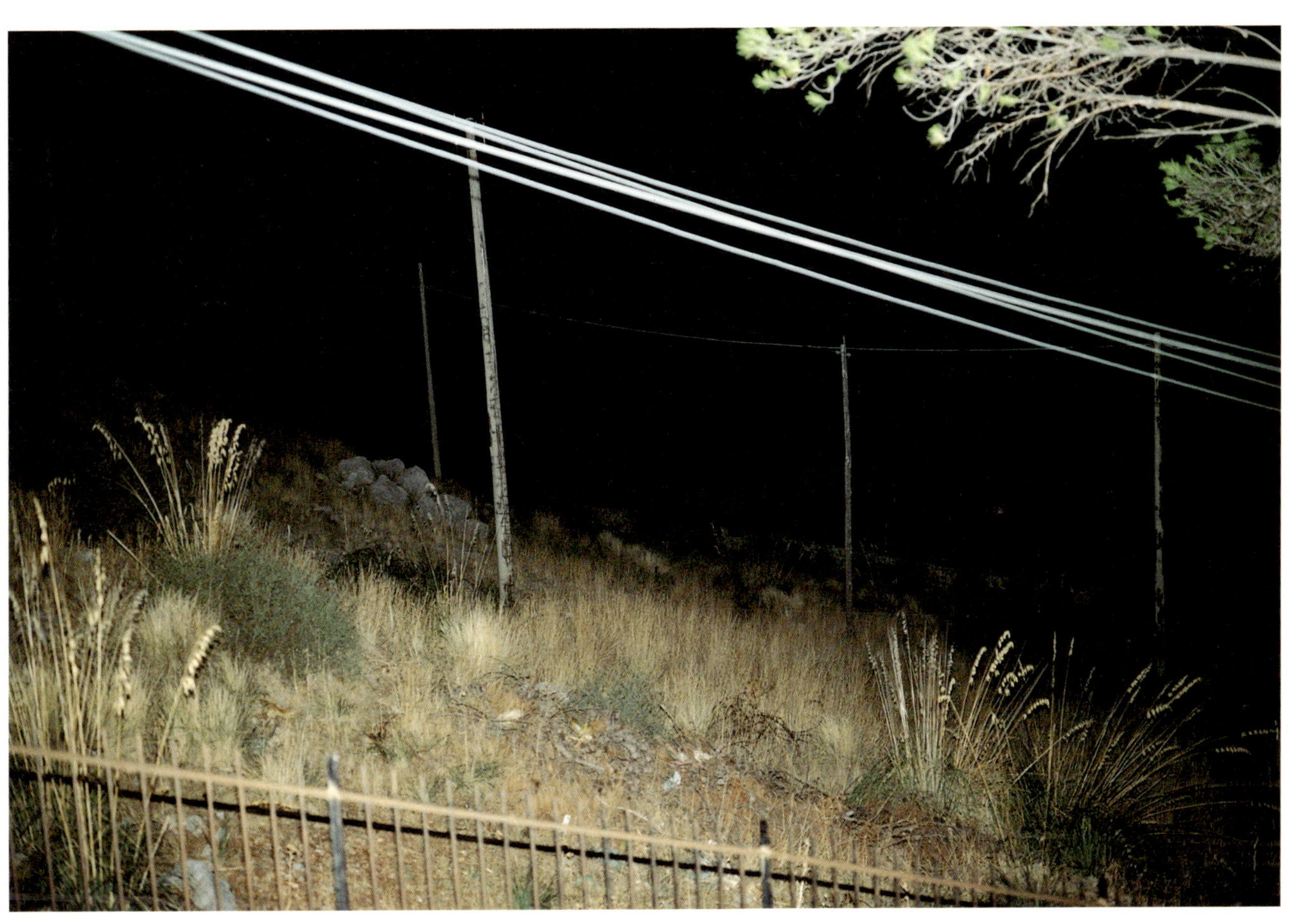

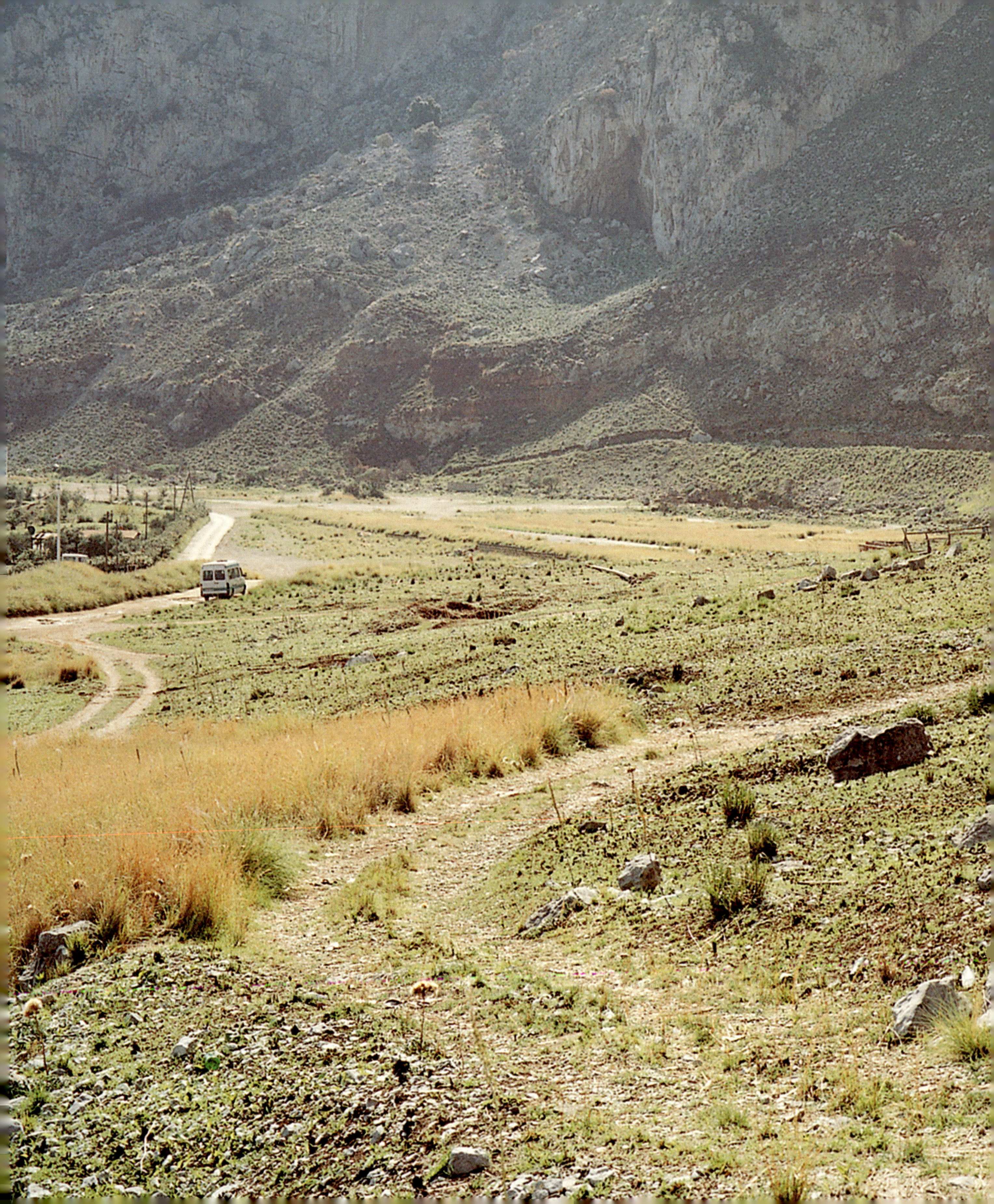

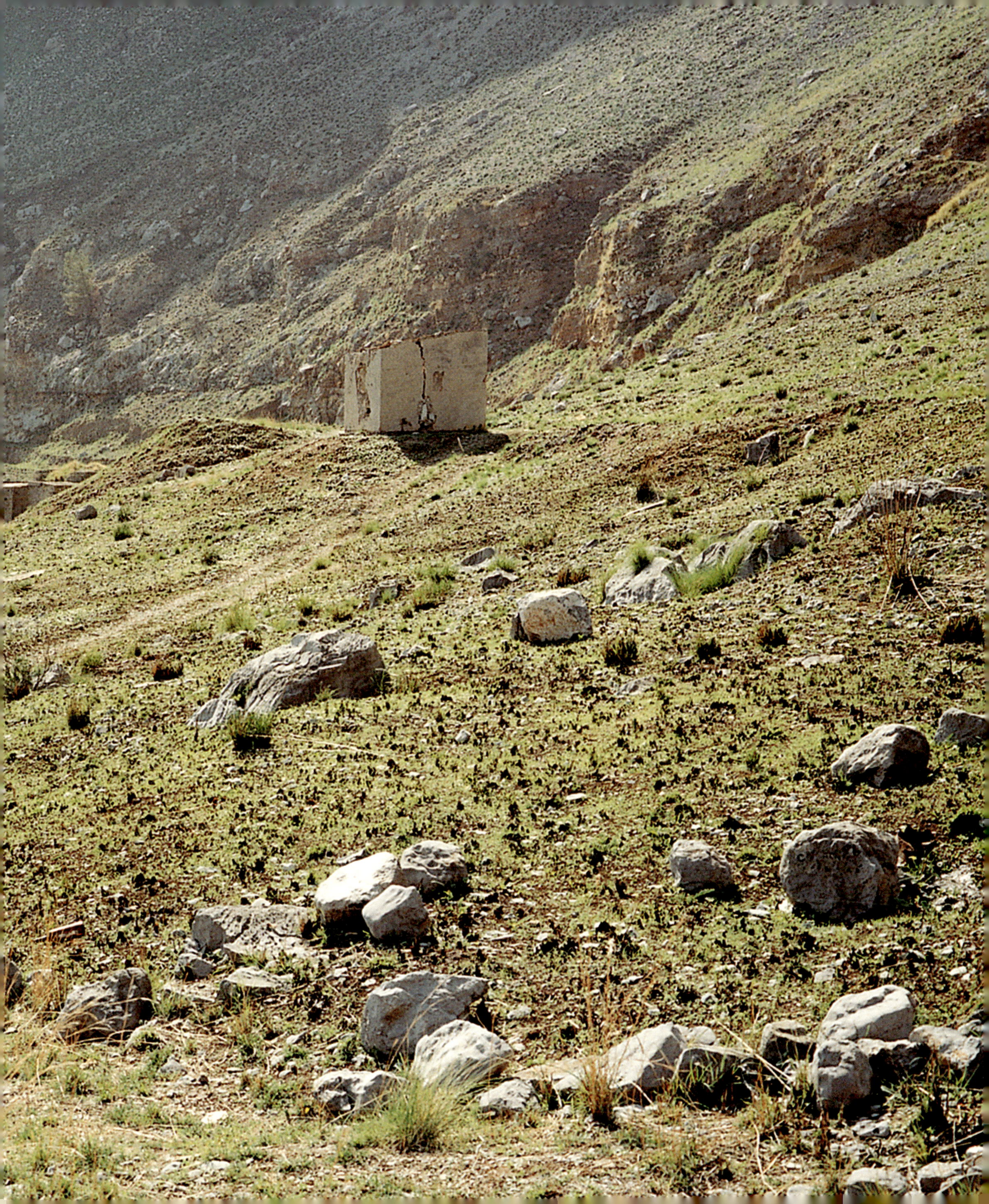

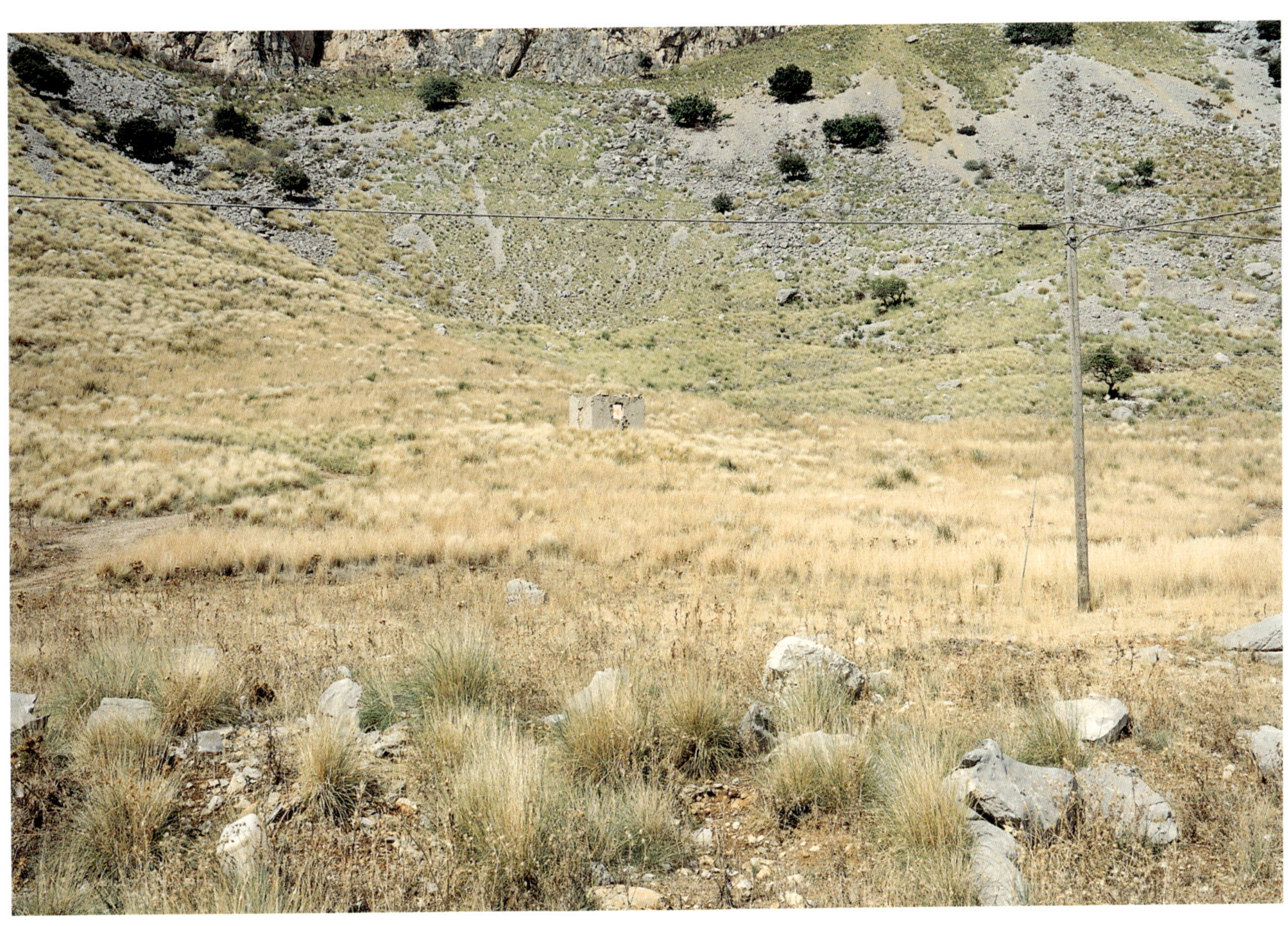

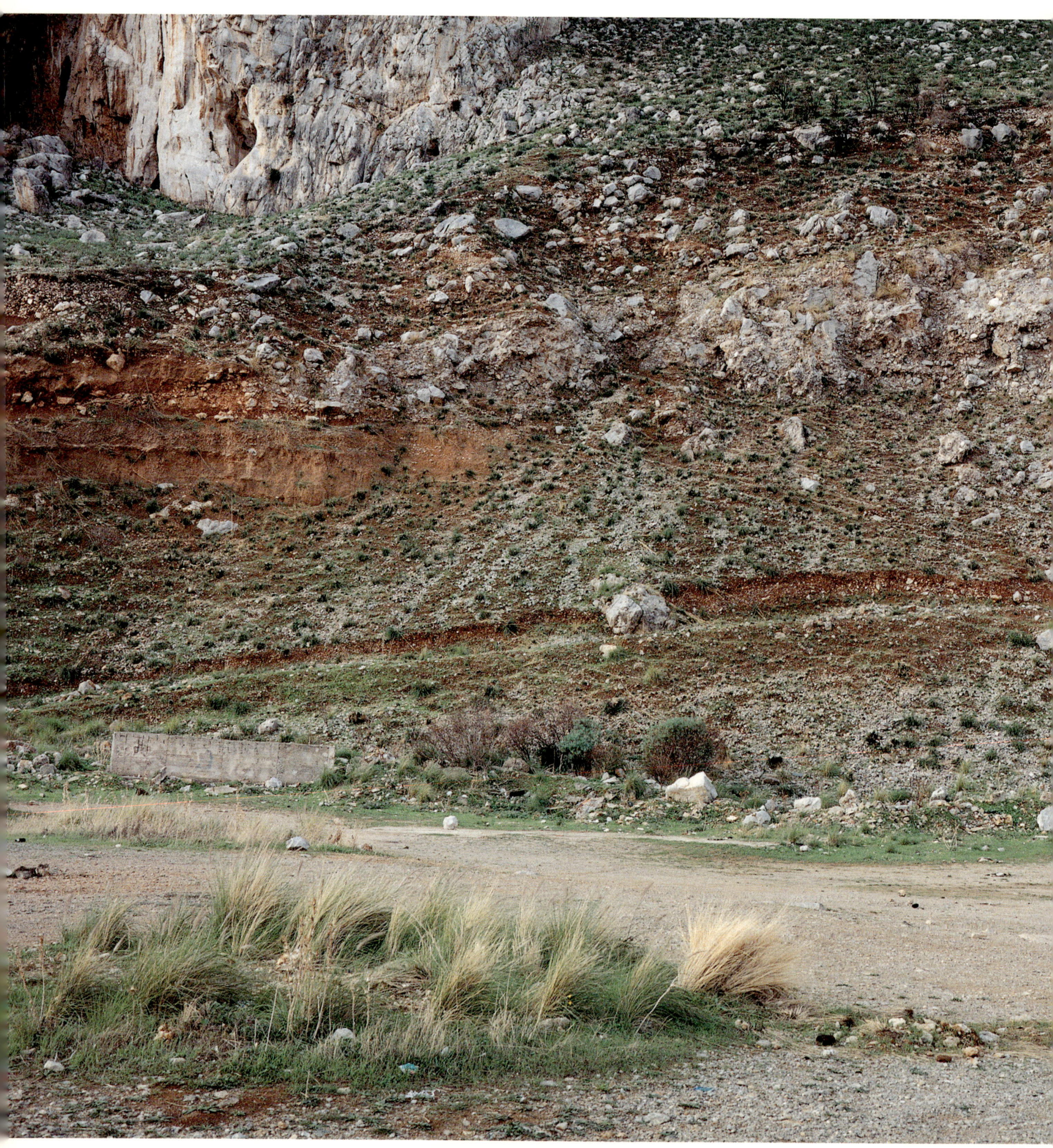

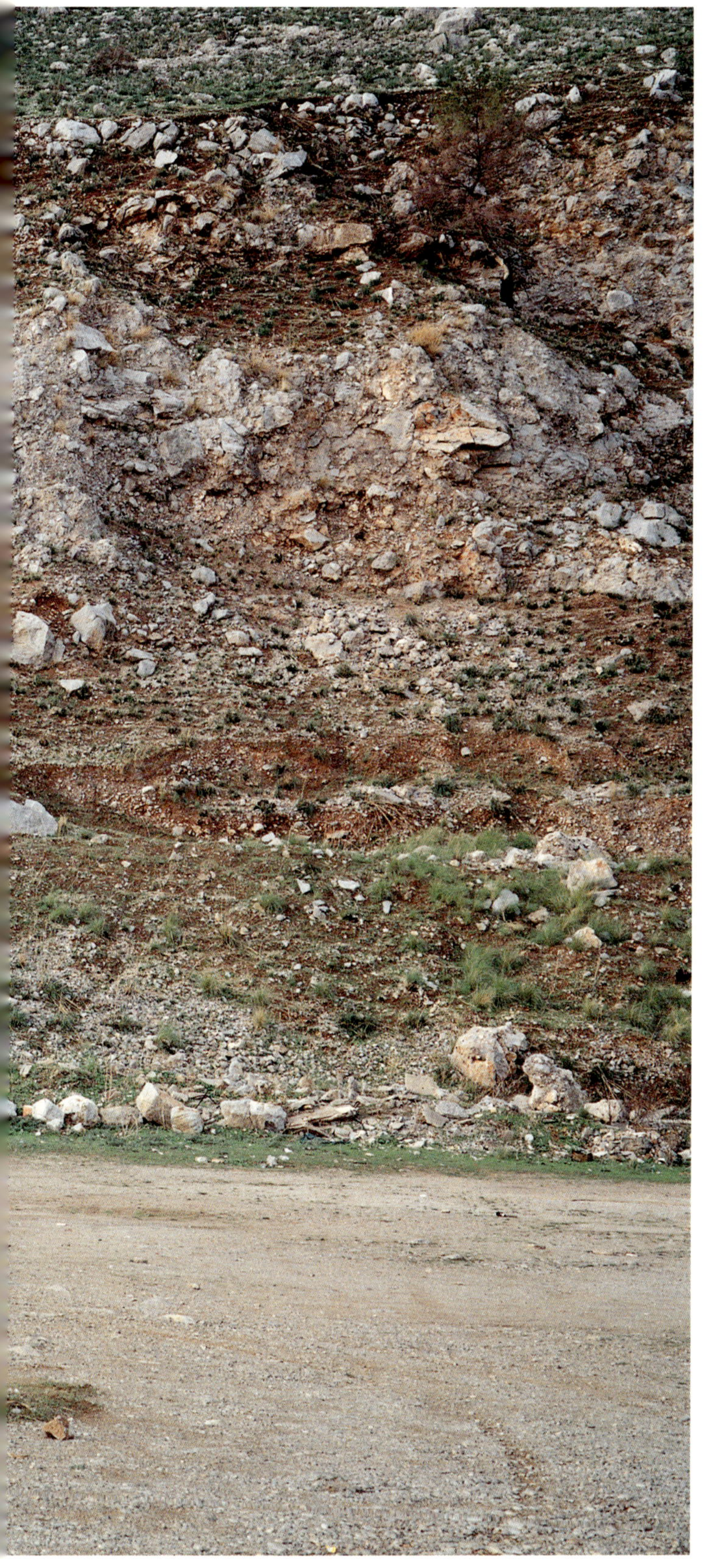

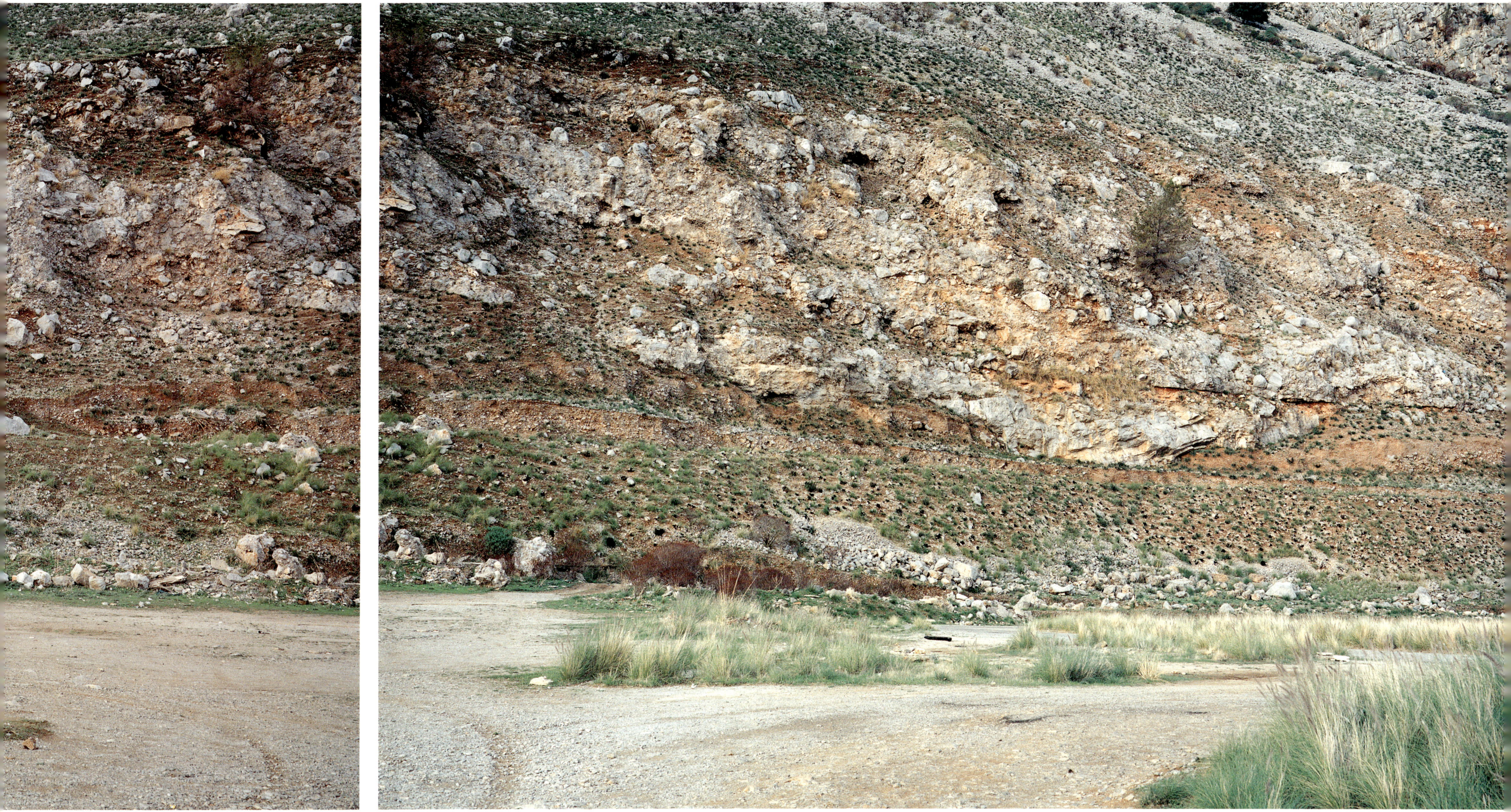

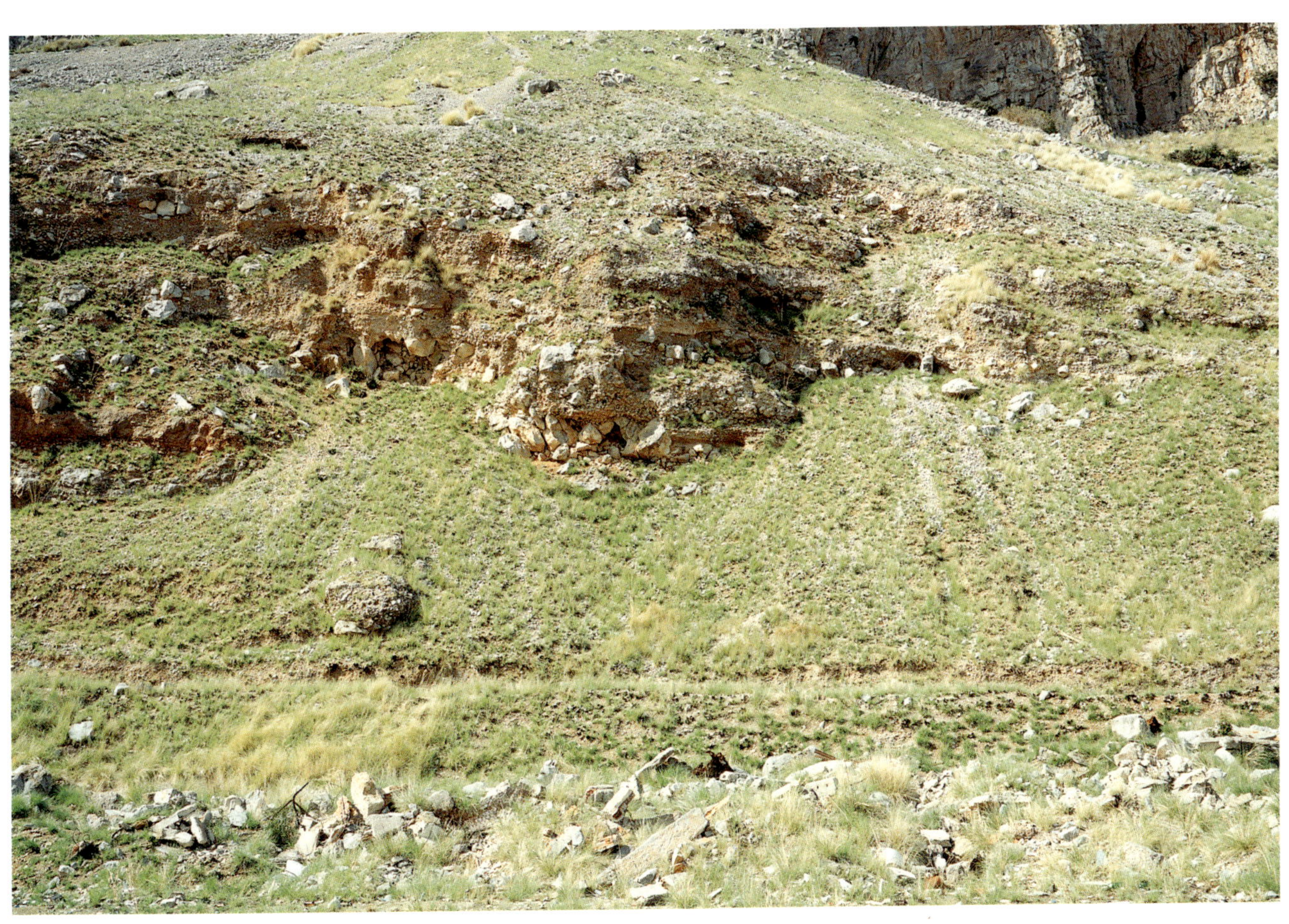

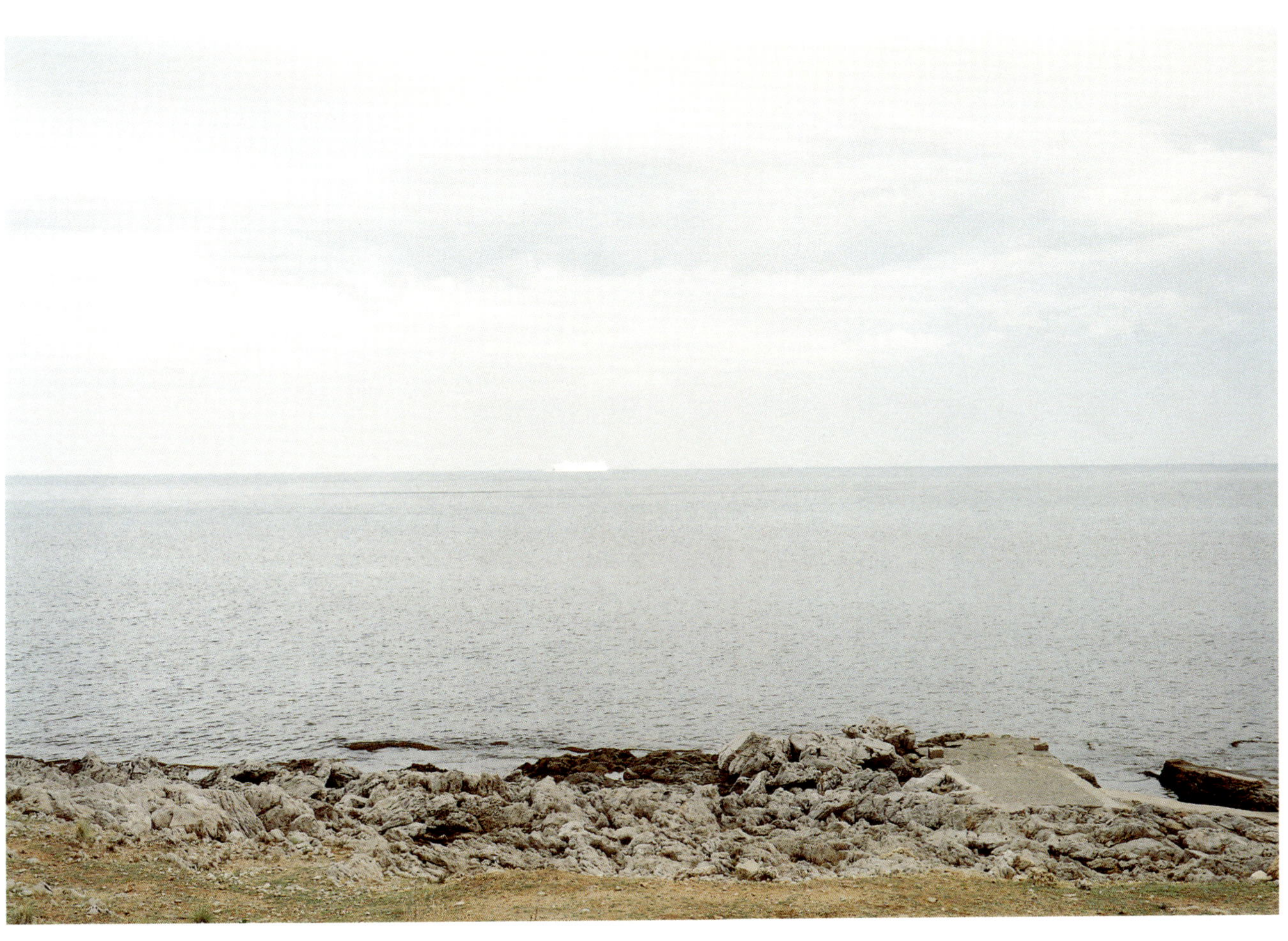

First published in 2002 by
Photoworks
Kent Institute of Art and Design
Oakwood Park
Maidstone ME16 8AG
U.K.

Tel: 01622 621134
Fax: 01622 621135
email: photo.works@virgin.net

PhotoWorks is an independent visual arts organisation that promotes photography within the South East of England, commissioning and producing new work over four main areas of activity: exhibitions, publications, research and education initiatives.



British Library Cataloguing - in - Publication Data
A catalogue record for this book is available from the British Library

ISBN 1-903796-03-2



Edited by David Chandler and Martin Cole
Designed by LOUP
Printed in Great Britain by Dexter Graphics Ltd

Distributed by
Cornerhouse Publications
70 Oxford Street
Manchester
M1 5NH
T: 0161 200 1503
F: 0161 200 1504
E: publications@cornerhouse.org

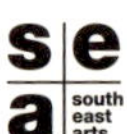

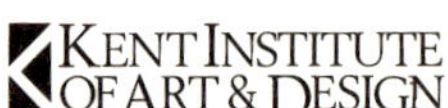


**Artist's Acknowledgements**

I would like to thank all those people who have given their help and advice during the making of this book, and especially Dean Pavitt for his excellent design, Adrian Cole for his writing, Peter Fraser for his printing, Xavier Ribas, Norman and Lesley Lewis for kindly looking over the book and Aithne Grayson for her ongoing input and point of view. Thanks also to David Chandler and Rebecca Drew of Photoworks for their continued commitment to the project and for helping to make the book possible.

Thanks to our Sicilian friends for their generosity, in particular Fabio Sgroi, Lorella Spedale, Monica Saitta, Georgio and Anna Mandala. And finally, thanks to the Giuseppe Pitre Museum of Ethnography in Palermo for permission to reproduce the bandit photographs.

Martin Cole